Saint-Simon and Saint-Simonism

SAINT-SIMON AND SAINT-SIMONISM.

BY THE SAME AUTHOR.

ROBERT OWEN, THE FOUNDER OF
SOCIALISM IN ENGLAND.

Small 8vo, 5s.

SAINT-SIMON AND SAINT-SIMONISM;

A CHAPTER IN THE

HISTORY OF SOCIALISM

IN FRANCE.

BY

ARTHUR JOHN BOOTH, M.A.

LONDON:
LONGMANS, GREEN, READER, AND DYER.
1871.

PRINTED BY TAYLOR AND CO.,
LITTLE QUEEN STREET, LINCOLN'S INN FIELDS.

PREFACE.

— · ✦ · —

THE interest that has been excited in England by the
Positive philosophy, must be my apology for publishing
the present volume. M. Comte has exercised a considerable influence in this country, although, as has been
frequently pointed out, some of the doctrines commonly
attributed to him are not original. I have here endeavoured to state the opinions of M. de Saint-Simon, with
whom M. Comte was early associated, in order to show
how far the pupil was indebted both for his truths and
for his errors to the teaching of his master. As the
writings of Saint-Simon are not likely to be very carefully studied, I have collected in an appendix numerous
extracts from them to substantiate the statements
made in the text. The inquiry is so purely technical
that it cannot be expected to prove very attractive.

The Saint-Simonian school, however, which caused
some ferment forty years ago has an interest of a dif-

ferent kind. Men who have since attained to eminence in various departments were connected with it; and some of the social and religious opinions now circulating freely amongst ourselves may there be seen in their infancy. The Saint-Simonians were among the earliest to advocate free trade through the press, and one of their disciples has been called the Cobden of France. They were likewise among the first to press the claims of women to political enfranchisement, and they maintained that some of the evils most injurious to society can only be removed by securing a greater freedom of divorce. They dwelt upon the injustice inflicted upon the majority of mankind in civilized communities by the inequalities of education and of fortune. The means by which they proposed to remove these artificial disabilities were highly impracticable; but the same result may be approximately attained in a different way, though at a time very distant from the present.

It seems now to be generally conceded that education should be extended even to the humblest member of the State; and if we remember that the standard is continually rising, we shall have good hope for the future. The vast disproportion of fortune and the rapid increase of poverty are more difficult problems. Yet even here there is no cause for despair. It cannot be long before the laws that artificially favour the accumulation of property in the hands of a few will be swept away; and much may be expected from the development of trade organizations, co-operative societies, and industrial partnerships. The growing intelligence of the masses may also check an undue increase of population; and enable them to perceive the folly of starving in a densely inhabited country, when wide regions of the earth remain uncultivated.

Nor are the religious opinions of the Saint-Simonians unrepresented in England. A dislike to dogmatic systems is not altogether unknown on the part of intelligent men; and there is a growing conviction that scientific inquiry is the only source of information respecting the formation of the universe and the origin and nature of man. The account that is generally accepted has been even regarded as mythological. Yet these and kindred questions are among the most important in theology; and if preference is given to the statements concerning them that are made by a Laplace or a Darwin, these persons and their successors are virtually theologians. If, therefore, as some appear to apprehend, a confidence in science should become universal, the existence of a scientific priesthood, as contemplated by Saint-Simon, however remote, is not impossible. It is evident also

that they would not be merely the exponents of natural
theology, but to some extent at least our religious and
moral teachers.   For the ideal of a religious life depends upon the conception we have formed concerning
the nature and destiny of man.   There are some
virtues, for example, that take their rise from the doctrine of the Fall and the conception of an offended
Deity; others, from the opinion that natural phenomena are guided by the direct interposition of Providence; and others, from the belief that death is the
commencement of a life for which it is our special duty
to prepare.   It is conceivable that some or all of these
views may be so far changed as to modify the virtues
or ideals to which they have given rise.   We may
hear less of the sinfulness of man, and more of the
advance he has made out of barbarism to civilization.
We may cease to quail before the wrath of Heaven,
and learn rather to admire the beauty and greatness of
its works.   We may discover that evil is more frequently the penalty of ignorance than of sin, and knowledge, not submission, is the remedy.   The profane
occupations of the world may be even invested with
dignity, and labour come to be valued as a virtue
at least not inferior to asceticism.   Now, men of
science will have much to do in this transformation.
Whose writings can so keenly excite religious emotion

as those that unfold the manifold mysteries of nature ?
Where else can we seek for the knowledge that will
lighten the evils by which our lives are beset ?   Who
can so well point out the way of life,. if that way is to
render profitable service to mankind upon earth ?
And if usefulness is a virtue and labour a religious
obligation, those who guide our efforts in these directions are in fact moral teachers.   Even the care of the
poor may likewise fall completely from the hands of
the clergy into those of lay officials.   And it is possible that these latter may be better versed in the
writings of Malthus or Fawcett, than in the precepts
of the Gospel or the traditions of the Church.   It will
be seen that the prospect, if brilliant, is not quite un-
clouded.   It cannot be supposed that any class can
view with much satisfaction its various functions thus
gradually passing away, by this process of unconscious
usurpation.

Already there exist in London two societies that
may be cited by some future historian as the beginning
of the Scientific Church.   One of these societies pro-
vides the public with a lecture on Sunday afternoon on
a purely secular subject.   The other holds its meeting
later in the day, and a selection of sacred music is its
principal attraction.   It is possible to imagine at some
distant period that these two societies have amalga--

mated. They meet no longer in a public hall, but in their own sacred edifice. It is an imposing building, upon which all the resources of art have been lavished. Its walls are adorned with pictures, and its aisles are decorated with statues of the great Heroes of Humanity; for no fear is now entertained that these may lead to an idolatrous worship. The service is conducted with solemnity; but there is neither creed nor catechism. It consists alone of sacred music, and as the heart is touched by its melody each worshipper pursues his own meditations in silence. When the oratorio is finished a lecturer ascends the pulpit, but his discourse is neither upon dogmatic theology, nor a dissertation of doubtful ethical value. As the musicians are chosen from among the most eminent artists of the day, so is the lecturer selected from the most distinguished men in the various departments of science; and his discourse will be upon the subjects with which he is best acquainted. The new church is regarded as a place of intellectual entertainment rather than as a new sect; and it is frequented by many of widely different theological opinions.

Again a long interval of time has elapsed, and the church that began in the metropolis has now extended to the other towns; and traces of its influence may be discerned in the country. A wiser and better instructed clergy has arisen. Their minds are no longer absorbed by disputes as to the colour of their vestments, nor even respecting their position at the altar. They are not only competent to teach their congregations some of the truths that are written in the great book of Nature; but such instruction forms a principal part of their discourses. Many of the divisions that now rend and endanger the church of Christ have been healed, and rival sects are united as though in the presence of a common enemy. Thus have the clergy regained their lost prestige, and the gulf that separates the lay and clerical minds has been lessened, for the conflict between Science and Theology, between Reason and Faith, has passed; and the day of reconciliation is at hand.

It is not impossible that the influence of Rationalism is still restricted to a small, though not unintelligent class; and that many reactions will long retard its general diffusion. Yet sufficient progress has already been made to render the conception of the Saint-Simonian religion intelligible; and it is hoped that an account of that strange sect, even as it is here imperfectly narrated, may not be altogether without interest.

LONDON, *April*, 1871.

PART I.

SAINT-SIMON.

SAINT-SIMON.

—◆—

"L'imagination des poëtes a placé l'âge d'or au berceau de l'espèce humaine, parmi l'ignorance et la grossièreté des premiers temps ; c'était bien plutôt l'âge de fer qu'il fallait y reléguer. L'âge d'or du genre humain n'est point derrière nous, il est au-devant ; il est dans la perfection de l'ordre social : nos pères ne l'ont point vu, nos enfants y arriveront un jour : c'est à nous de leur en frayer la route."—*Saint-Simon.*

THE name of Count Henry de Saint-Simon has attracted far more attention since his death than during his life. It has become associated with a singular sect of religious and social innovators, who entertained the Parisians, for a few years, with long beards and grotesque costumes, and concerning whose morality certain sinister rumours were current.

English readers, who are not very curious in such matters, probably heard of him for the first time in connection with M. Comte, and the impression produced was probably unfavourable. His disciples have claimed for him the merit of being the founder of the Positive Philosophy, while those of Comte declare that he was incapable of even understanding it. It may therefore be of some service to give an account of this eccentric writer, so that the reader may be better qualified to judge of the merits of the controversy.

Claude Henri de Rouvroy, Comte de Saint-Simon, was born at Paris, in 1760. His family claims to be one of the noblest in France. It pretends to a descent from Charlemagne, by the marriage of a remote ancestor with a daughter of the House of Vermandois. It attained distinction so early as the battle of Agincourt, where one of its members fell. Subsequently it has divided into several branches; Claude Henri belonged to that of the Marquis of Sandricourt, and he would have been heir to the great Duc de Saint-Simon, but this inheritance was forfeited by his father through a quarrel with the duke.[1] Two of his uncles were men of note. One, the Marquis of Saint-Simon, lived at Utrecht, and published several works on botanical and historical subjects. Another was Bishop of Agde, and perished in 1791, during the Revolution.

Saint-Simon displayed the peculiarities of his character from an early age. At thirteen he refused to go to his first communion. His father for this offence sent him to prison, but Claude overpowered the

---

[1] "Le duché-pairie, la grandesse d'Espagne et 500,000 livres de rentes dont jouissait le duc de Saint-Simon, devaient passer sur ma tête. Il s'est brouillé avec mon père, qu'il a déshérité." He adds, "J'ai donc perdu les titres et la fortune du duc de Saint-Simon, mais j'ai hérité de sa passion pour la gloire."

keeper and effected his escape. Upon another occasion, he was bitten by a mad dog; he at once procured a pistol, and determined to commit suicide upon the first symptoms of hydrophobia. His conduct in youth was extravagant and dissipated, and he in consequence incurred the displeasure of his father,[2] yet in the midst of his excesses he never lost sight of ambition. "Levez-vous, Monsieur le Comte; vous avez de grandes choses à faire;" it was thus, at the age of seventeen, that he desired his servant to call him in the morning. He had just then entered the army, and two years afterwards he went to America, where he served with distinction throughout five campaigns. He was present at the siege of York and the surrender of Lord Cornwallis, and received the order of Cincinnatus, for the bravery he displayed upon these occasions. He had the misfortune to be on board the 'Ville de Paris' at the time of her capture by Rodney. A ball struck him, which, without depriving him of consciousness, prevented him from manifesting any signs of life; in this state he had a narrow escape of being thrown overboard. At the

[2] He writes from America, "J'espère, mon cher papa et ami, que 'arrangement que j'ai mis dans mes petites affaires depuis un an vous aura fait oublier les étourderies que j'avais faites. M. le Marquis de Saint-Simon sera à même de vous dire la conduite qu'il m'a vu tenir pour vous forcer de me rendre votre amitié, que ma jeunesse m'avait fait perdre en partie. Je ne veux pas regretter le temps perdu, mais bien le réparer de mon mieux." — *Œuvres de Saint-Simon et d'Enfantin*, 2nd ed. Paris: Dentu. 1865–9. 23 vols. Vol. i. p. 5.

1783. end of the war he returned to France; he was made Chevalier of St Louis, and colonel of the regiment of Aquitaine. He was then only twenty-three years of age, and possessed an ardent desire for knowledge. When quartered at Metz, he took the opportunity of attending the lectures of Monge, the celebrated mathematician. The army had been distasteful to him from the first, but now, in time of peace, it became quite unendurable; he accordingly left it, and proceeded to travel. He visited Holland first, and afterwards Spain. At this period his mind was chiefly directed to scientific subjects. When he was in Mexico, before his return to Europe, he communicated to the Vice-roy a plan he had formed, with a view to unite the Atlantic to the Pacific. When in Spain, he undertook to open a communication with the sea from Madrid, by means of a canal. He was only prevented from attempting this design by the events which unexpectedly recalled him to France. He returned to that country in November, 1789, to watch the progress of the Revolution, and was elected President of the commune of Falvy, in Péronne, where his property was situated. In his address to the electors, he declared his resolution to renounce the title of Count, as he considered it to be inferior to that of citizen. He frequently addressed the people in the parish church in favour of liberty and equality. He refused the office of Maire, lest it might be thought that he owed it to his rank. But if, in public, he affected to despise the advantages of birth, he was careful to secure those of wealth. He entered into a partnership with M. de Redern, the Prussian ambassador to England, with the view of speculating in church lands. They purchased the whole of the national property situated in the Département de l'Orne, besides some magnificent hotels in Paris. The enormous depreciation in the value of assignats greatly facilitated these acquisitions, the value of which amounted, it is said, to eight millions of francs. In addition to this, they jointly established a manufactory which they conducted with success. Their proceedings were at length interrupted, and their lives exposed to some danger, during the ascendancy of Robespierre. M. de Redern escaped from France, but Saint-Simon was thrown into prison, where he remained for eleven months. During that period he reflected deeply on the political problems of the time, and his ancestor Charlemagne appeared to him in a vision. " Mon fils," said the apparition, " tes succès comme philosophe égaleront ceux que j'ai obtenus comme militaire et politique." So soon as he was released from prison, he determined to renounce further speculation, and to apply himself exclusively to realize this magnificent prophecy. " He had sought fortune," he says, " merely as a means to organize a great industrial establishment, to found an advanced

1797. scientific school,—in a word, to contribute to the progress of knowledge, and to the amelioration of the lot of mankind." He had fancied that M. de Redern was inspired by equally exalted motives. That gentleman possessed large estates in Saxony, upon which he had abolished serfdom and feudal rights. His views were extremely liberal, and for a time the two partners got on very well together, but the withdrawal of Saint-Simon was the commencement of a quarrel between them which led to much recrimination. M. de Redern would not grant more than a sum of 144,000 francs, and, for some reason, Saint Simon could not enforce more favourable terms. With that, however, he retired and devoted himself at once to study. He delighted to collect together artists and men of letters and science, and to receive instruction from their conversation. Lagrange, Monge, and Berthollet were his frequent companions. He liberally assisted indigent men of letters, and undertook the delivery of a gratuitous course of lectures. He took an apartment opposite the Polytechnic School, and recommenced, at the age of thirty-eight, his scientific education. He pursued the study of mathematical physics for three years, and then removed to an apartment adjoining the Medical School, in order to follow with attention the lectures on physiology. While engaged in this manner, he thought it necessary to become acquainted with various forms of life. He accordingly resorted

to places of evil repute, and might even be seen in
the company of persons of blemished character. His
enemies accused him of immorality, but he always
defended himself from the charge on the ground that
he was merely pursuing philosophical investigation.[3]

At length, in 1801, he married; his resources could
not long support his increased expenses. Accordingly
he procured a divorce from his wife, not on account of
any incompatibility of disposition, for he was deeply
affected by the ceremony, but that he might secure an
alliance more suited to his poverty. At that time
Madame de Staël was a widow; she enjoyed a competent income, and Saint-Simon conceived the idea that
a marriage with her would be highly advantageous.
He thereupon presented himself at Coppet, but unfortunately Madame de Staël did not view the matter
in the same light, and his effort was unsuccessful.[4] It
was during his visit to Geneva that he published his

---

[3] "Je dis que mes actions ne doivent pas être jugées d'après les
mêmes principes que celles du commun des hommes, parce que ma vie,
jusqu'à ce jour, a été un cours d'expériences. . . . Si je vois un homme
qui ne s'occupe pas de science générale, fréquenter les maisons de jeu et
de débauche, voilà un homme qui se perd. Mais, si cet homme s'occupe
de philosophie théorique, . . . je dirai : cet homme parcourt la carrière
du vice dans une direction qui le conduira nécessairement à la plus haute
vertu. . . . Mon estime pour moi a toujours augmenté dans la proportion du tort que j'ai fait à ma réputation." — *Œuvres*, vol. xvii.
p. 86.

[4] It is said that he expressed himself to her in these curious terms :
—" Madame, vous êtes la femme la plus extraordinaire du monde,
comme j'en suis l'homme le plus extraordinaire : à nous deux, nous
ferions sans doute un enfant encore plus extraordinaire."

1803. first pamphlet. It appeared in 1803 under the title, 'Lettres d'un Habitant de Genève à ses Contemporains.' In it Saint-Simon proposed to re-establish order in society, by means of a union between the intellectual classes and the territorial proprietors, with a view to suppress the authority recently acquired by the ignorant people, and to which the horrors of the French revolution may be justly ascribed.[5] The model proposed for imitation is the middle ages. At that period the clergy were possessed of all the available knowledge, and through their alliance with the feudal aristocracy the people found themselves constrained in mind and body, with the beneficial result that social order was undisturbed. Since then, however, a very important change has taken place, by which the clergy have lost their spiritual ascendancy. The great advance that has been made in physical science has totally revolutionized our views of man and nature; and the clergy, instead of embodying each new discovery into their systems, and themselves leading the way towards the further acquisition of knowledge, have remained immovable in positions that have become untenable. They have not only in this manner lost their title to be considered the intellectual guides and authorities of men, but they have actually assumed an attitude of hostility to progress. Thus there has

[5] 'Saint-Simon, sa Vie et ses Travaux,' par M. G. Hubbard. Paris: Guillaumin. 1857. Page 138.

arisen the direst anarchy in society. On the one hand, there is a class of men whose authority is supposed by the ignorant to be derived from heaven; upon the other, an increasing body of investigators, whose discoveries are directly opposed to the doctrines of the authorized teachers. Now, what constituted the strength of the spiritual power during the middle ages was the circumstance that scientific knowledge was then in complete harmony with theological belief. The only means of restoring the spiritual authority that has been lost by disunion, and without which social order is impossible, is to re-establish the harmony between theology and science; and this is not to be accomplished, as has been vainly attempted, by arresting the progress of knowledge, but by advancing theology so as to meet the new requirements of science. In Saint-Simonian phraseology the periods during which social order is firmly established, by the harmony between knowledge and belief, are designated *organic*, while those in which knowledge is gradually undermining the foundations of the popular creed are called *critical*.

Now, the special characteristic of the present state of knowledge is the total elimination from nature of all providential interference, and the submission of all phenomena whatsoever to the reign of law. Indeed, according to Saint-Simon, the several laws of nature may be reduced to one general law—that of gravitation. It is, of course, evident that such a result must seriously affect a theology which depends for its authority upon reputed miracle, and counsels prayer to a Being who it imagines may be induced, by supplication, to modify the established order of nature.

In truth, the sources of our knowledge are imagination and observation. In the childhood of intellect the imagination prevails, but it is gradually corrected according as facts are more and more observed. To this process is due the elimination of astrology from astronomy, and of alchemy from chemistry. Each science is freed from its purely imaginative elements in the order of its simplicity; that is to say, according as its phenomena are easy or difficult of observation. Now physiology is the most complex of all the sciences, and therefore, it is not unnatural that it should still be encumbered with much speculation that is solely due to the imagination, and has no foundation in fact. But the time has at length arrived when its deliverance should be wrought; and the classes who indulge in vain speculations concerning man—such as theologians, metaphysicians, and others—should be entirely superseded by men of science, whose knowledge has alone any reliable foundation. During the period in human history, when the imagination predominated, the opinions of the clergy respecting man and nature were in strict accordance with the then state of knowledge, and they, therefore, were the spiritual classes, but it is otherwise now. It is to the scientific classes that we must look for our information upon these subjects; and hence they have in reality taken the place formerly occupied by the clergy, and should be formally substituted for them.

Such being the general principles laid down by Saint-Simon, he proceeds to suggest how they should be carried out into practice.

Gravitation being assumed to be the ultimate law of the universe, Newton, its discoverer, is entitled to the honour of founder of the New Religion. Mausoleums will be erected to him in the Temples which will be dedicated to his worship. For he is seated, it appears, at the right hand of God and directs the progress of knowledge. He exercises authority over the inhabitants of all the planets; and, therefore, his worship should be conducted in a style adapted to his importance. The priests who serve at his altars will be men of science, and attached to each temple there will be a college. The text-books of science will become the text-books of theology, for it is only by science that we can attain to any true knowledge respecting the subject-matter of theology. The Council of Newton will be composed of twenty-one persons, who will be called the Elect of Humanity. Their functions will be scientific inquiry and a general supervision of the Scientific Religion, while its ceremonial will be directed by scholars and artists. The Elect of

1803. Humanity will be excluded from all political office, and will be maintained by means of a public subscription.[6] Each subscriber of either sex will have the power to nominate a candidate, who will be elected by a majority of votes, and for one year. Women are eligible. In this manner theology, which powerfully affects the masses, will be brought once more into complete accordance with knowledge; and the division that at present exists in the spiritual power, to the great diminution of its authority, will terminate.

The moral duty of labour will be rigidly enforced upon all. "Tous les hommes doivent travailler" is the motto of the new faith; and will admit of no exceptions. Those who cannot work with their heads must work with their hands. Society will be composed of three classes. The Spiritual Power—or the control of opinion—in the hands of the learned. The Temporal Power—or the control of the State—in the hands of the territorial proprietors, and the right of election to the high offices of Humanity in the hands of all who contribute to their maintenance. Such was the work with which Saint-Simon sought to captivate the mistress of Coppet. The pretensions he put forward were truly magnificent. He claimed the honours of a prophet:—" C'est Dieu qui m'a parlé;

---

[6] "L'humanité ne doit pas perdre de vue qu'elle doit récompenser les hommes qui lui servent de flambeaux, et qu'elle doit collectivement récompenser ceux de ces flambeaux qui sont assez lumineux pour éclairer toute la terre."—*Hubbard*, p. 121.

un homme aurait-il pu inventer une religion supérieure
à toutes celles qui ont existé ?" It may, however, be
remarked of him that, unlike most prophets, he did
not deceive himself. He was far from being a religious enthusiast. His education had been directed by
D'Alembert, he had enjoyed the society of Rousseau,
he had been the admirer of Franklin, and he remained
true to the traditions of his youth.[7] He sent a copy of
the 'Lettres' to the Citoyen Premier Consul, but it
is to be feared it never reached its destination.[8] The
work attracted no attention among the public; indeed
it appears at a later period to have been regarded with
but little favour by its author. He was never known
to speak of it, and after his death his intimate friend
and disciple, Olinde Rodrigue, edited a later work
under the impression that it was the first.[9] Before
his visit to Geneva he had crossed over to England
and now he made a short excursion to Germany previous to his return to Paris, but his pecuniary resources
were soon exhausted. The unsuccessful issue of his
matrimonial scheme had not been repaired by literary success. He was, in fact, reduced to the verge

1803.

---

[7] He confessed afterwards, 1812 ('Œuvres,' vol. xvii. p. 130), "Je
ne suis point un illuminé: mes déterminations ne me paraissent pas
avoir été dictées par l'Être suprême."

[8] The letter and copy were bought at a public sale sixty years afterwards by one of his disciples; so says his latest biographer. (' Œuvres,
vol. i. p. 23, note. Compare vol. xvii. p. 7, note.)

[9] Hubbard, p. 38, note.

of starvation, and obliged to seek employment. After
some delay the Comte de Ségur appointed him a
copyist at the Mont de Piété, where he received a
salary of 1000 francs, or £40 a year, for nine hours'
work a day. At the end of six months, however, he
was rescued from this deplorable position by the kind-
ness of Diard, who had been his valet in the days of
his prosperity. M. Diard permitted him to reside in
his house, and even supplied him with the means of
publishing his next work. It appeared in 1807 and
1808, with the title, ' Introduction aux Travaux Scientifiques du XIXme Siècle.' Napoleon had demanded an
account of the progress of science since 1789. This
work was intended to be an answer to the inquiry.
It was conceived upon so large a scale that ten years
would be required to complete it. The first volume
was to treat of inorganic and organic science, and of
philosophy. The second would criticize the ' Histoire
de l'Esprit Humain,' by Condorcet, and supply an
' Esquisse d'un Nouveau Tableau Historique,' divided
into nine epochs. The third volume was intended to
contain a plan for a new encyclopedia. Saint-Simon
can scarcely be said to have attempted the execution
of this ambitious project.

What he has actually written consists of two parts.
The first treats exclusively of scientific method. It
endeavours to show that the mind adopts alternately
the synthetic or *à priori*, and the analytic or *à pos-*

teriori methods.[10] With this view he enters into an 1808. elaborate historical appreciation of the method pursued in philosophy, science, and criticism from the time of Bacon to the present day. The works of Bacon and Descartes, he says, are synthetical, those of Locke and Newton analytical.[11] It is now necessary for us to abandon the latter, and to return once more to the synthetic or *à priori* method.[12] The second part of his book is less elaborate, and more interesting; it consists of a series of detached essays, or more properly speaking of notes, which the author has published from his commonplace book, without giving himself the trouble to elaborate, or even to connect together. Indeed, he lays no claim to lite-

[10] 'Œuvres Choisies de Saint-Simon.' Bruxelles. 1859. 3 vols. Vol. i. p. 66.

[11] "Bacon a adopté la marche synthétique ; il s'est placé au point de vue scientifique général. Descartes a suivi l'impulsion donnée par ce novateur en philosophie générale ; il a procédé par voie de synthèse." "Locke et Newton ont pris une nouvelle direction ; ils ont cherché des faits et ils en ont trouvé de capitaux."—*Ib.* pp. 58, 67.

[12] "L'École est devenue Newto-Lockiste : depuis près d'un siècle elle suit la direction que ces deux grands hommes lui ont donnée ; elle s'occupe de la recherche des faits, et elle néglige les théories. Pour progrès de la science, l'Institut devrait travailler au perfectionnement la théorie, il devrait revenir à la direction de Descartes."—*Ib.* p. 58. "Je vois que l'influence exercée par les mânes de Newton est très-nuisible aux progrès de la science, et je crie de toutes mes forces à mes contemporains ; il est temps de changer de route, c'est sur la route *à priori* qu'il y a, dans ce moment, des découvertes à faire."—*Ib.* p. 164. By comparing this opinion with that expressed five years before, in the 'Lettres de Genève,' the reader will be able to judge of Saint-Simon's inconsistency.

rary merit; he leaves to professional authors the task of reproducing his ideas in a systematic form/ For himself, he writes merely in the character of a gentleman, of a descendant of the Comtes of Vermandois, as the inheritor of the pen of the Duc de Saint-Simon. At the origin of our race, he says, the difference between man and other animals was scarcely perceptible, yet man enjoyed a slight superiority in physical organization, and to it the possibility of civilization is due, as well as all the moral and intellectual qualities that have been since developed. Not till the formation of signs, oral and written, could even the line of demarcation be clearly traced between intellect and instinct. There is such an entire absence of any inherent difference between the two, that if the human race were to disappear from the earth, the species next in rank would speedily supply its place and rival its intelligence. As regards the history of the race itself, it is precisely analogous to the life of the individual: we can trace it through its infancy and manhood; we can predict its old age and death. The child is amused with toys, and builds mounds of sand by the sea-shore; similarly the Egyptian civilizations reared huge pyramids of stone. The young man delights in poetry and art; the Greeks produced one poem of unrivalled excellence, and have left art treasures of peerless beauty. Later he becomes warlike; the Romans subjugated the earth. And then his

activity diminishes, and as he approaches forty-five 1808.
years of age he seeks repose, he delights in speculation, and the tranquil pleasures of industry. We have
nearly entered upon that stage. Inasmuch, then, as
the race is exactly 8000 years upon the earth, we may
conclude that one year in the life of man corresponds
to 200 in the duration of mankind; and hence, by an
arithmetical process, we can tell precisely how long
the race has yet to exist. And here, according to
Saint-Simon, is the capital error of Condorcet: he
overlooked the exact parallel between man and mankind, and he was, in consequence, led to predict the
perfectibility of the latter. He thus forgot its necessary period of decrepitude. Nor can it be said that the
progress of humanity, in some respects, is unaccompanied by a corresponding retrogression in others.
If the full-grown man gains in experience, he loses in
enthusiasm; if his reason is strengthened, his imagination is weakened. For these reasons, we, in our
maturity, cannot approach the Greeks in poetry and
art, the works of our youth. The 'Philosophes Cir-
culaires' are betrayed into a still more glaring error:
according to them the human mind continues to
rotate in a circle, consequently in time it returns to the
point from whence it set out; and, in the course of its
movement, it has already described several revolutions; or, to adopt the favourite expression of this
class of thinkers, "History repeats itself." How far

such an opinion is removed from the truth may be seen by a study of the successive evolutions through which religious thought has passed.

At first the mind believed in many independent causes; it then adopted the idea of numerous agents of a single Cause or Intelligence. Afterwards it rose to the conception of a Unique and Universal Cause, which is called God; but now it has perceived that the relation between God and the universe is incomprehensible and unimportant. It has, therefore, applied itself to the discovery of facts, and it asserts that the most general fact it can arrive at must be the one cause of all phenomena. The first of these phases corresponds to the civilization of the Egyptians; the second was introduced by Homer, when he charged Olympus with the government of the universe; the third is to be attributed to Socrates, who invented God;[18] while the fourth is the work of Descartes. Now the reader must not fail to observe that Saint-Simon attributes each successive idea to the invention of a philosopher. Pure when it first emanates from his brain, it becomes vulgarized as it descends to the people. Thus, while there has been a continuous progress among philosophers,—ascending as they have done from the rudimentary conception of fetishism to

---

[18] 'Œuvres Choisies,' vol. i. p. 206. Elsewhere (p. 189) he says, Moses also invented God; indeed, he adds, the idea probably arose spontaneously in several nations.

the entire elimination of all supernatural agency,—the   1808.
people have accepted each new idea, and afterwards
adapted it to suit their inferior intelligence. It is
evident, therefore, that as the idea of God was totally
destroyed by Descartes, and has been since replaced
by an Ultimate Law, it is necessary that this conception be in time corrupted down to the level of a religion, in order that it may become comprehensible to
the vulgar: for religion is merely the application of the
prevailing scientific opinion, and its chief use is as an
instrument by which the enlightened may govern the
ignorant.[14] The new theology will receive the name
of Physicism, and it will be in complete accordance
with the most recent discoveries; its catechism will
be in fact a succinct compendium of the Encyclopedia.
Yet the transition will not be rapid: Deism is still useful as a political engine, and a belief in it should therefore be professed in public. Indeed, it is almost inevitable that two distinct methods of thought should
exist at the same historic period—the one entertained
by the enlightened, the other by the ignorant. It is
evident, in the present instance at least, that the
people are not yet prepared to discard Theism. "I
believe," he says, "in the necessity of a religion for
the maintenance of social order; I believe that the

[14] "La religion est la collection des applications de la science générale,
au moyen desquelles les hommes éclairés gouvernent les hommes igno-
rants."—Œuvres Choisies, p. 213.

system of Deism has become effete; I believe that
Physicism is not yet sufficiently established to serve
as the basis for a religion; I believe that two distinct
doctrines must exist,—the one, Physicism for the educated, the other, Deism for the ignorant.   It is easy to
demonstrate that the human mind has progressed
during the last few centuries in direct proportion to
the decline in the belief in God."[15] And here we should
be upon our guard against an error into which Condorcet has fallen; for, although the advance in our
scientific knowledge has necessarily led to a complete
change in our theology, we should never forget the
services rendered to mankind by the Catholic clergy.
It was they who cultivated the ground, and converted unhealthy marshes into fertile land; it was
they who preserved and interpreted manuscripts, who
conducted the education of the laity, who studied
metaphysics and the sciences, who founded the first
hospitals. Talent always obtains its recompense. From
the seventh to the fourteenth century the clergy were
abundantly rewarded; if they have since then forfeited power and riches, it is because they have been
excelled by the laity in knowledge and general utility.

This work is enlivened by a few remarkable scientific
discoveries,—amongst others, that America rising out
of the sea was the cause of the Deluge; that the earth
was entirely covered with water when it passed from

1808.

the condition of a comet to that of a planet; that animal production, and indeed mental production, proceed
from convulsions of nature. Thus whales, which are the
largest animals, are also the most ancient, and date
from a period when nature was the most vehemently convulsed. He anticipates some great intellectual result
from the upheaving of the Revolution. It will be remembered that in the ' Lettres de Genève ' he excluded the
learned class from direct participation in the government; he now recommends that they be admitted to
the offices of State. He says, " The people are always
restless, and they will always be so when there ceases
to be due proportion between the knowledge and the
power of the governing classes, and the ignorance and
dependence of the governed."[16] Consequently he ar-
gues that the system founded by Napoleon, in Italy,
was the best the world had ever seen, for power was
given both to the learned and to the proprietors. The
great power is the power of intellect. The learned
classes and artists possess this power in an eminent degree; they should therefore become part of the governing body, for the object of government is to keep the
ignorant in dependence upon the higher classes.

Saint-Simon prohibited the public sale of this tract,
lest it might be injurious to the ignorant. Only 100
copies were printed, which he distributed among a few
discreet persons whose intellects were sufficiently de-

[16] ' Œuvres Choisies,' vol. i. p. 210.

1808. veloped to appreciate its merits without being injured
by its contents.

His next work, 'Lettres au Bureau des Longitudes,'
is, to a great extent, a repetition of the preceding. He
wrote nothing of any importance for some years. In
the meantime he lost his faithful friend Diard, and
was once more reduced to a state of destitution.
Accordingly he had recourse to M. de Redern in the
hope of obtaining assistance from him. " Du pain et
des livres, voilà tout ce que vous demande votre ancien
ami, qui reconnaît avoir eu bien des torts vis-à-vis de
vous, de sa famille et de tout le monde, mais qui se
sent les moyens de réparer ses torts vis-à-vis de vous,
de sa famille et de tout le monde si vous lui donnez
des livres indispensables et du pain." A very long
printed correspondence ensued, but with the exception
of a donation of 500 francs, Saint-Simon did not gain
anything by it; indeed he acknowledged that M. de
Redern had law upon his side, if not equity. Saint-
Simon's family at length volunteered to give him a
small pension, but it was not sufficient to remove him
above want. Afterwards he received from Carnot the
appointment of Sub-librarian to the Bibliothèque de
l'Arsenal, which he however only retained till the
second fall of Napoleon. His disastrous position however, in no way impaired the courageous energy of his
intellect. In 1813 he wrote his 'Mémoire sur la
Science de l'Homme.' This work he could not afford

to print, but he made sixty manuscript copies of it, and distributed them among men occupying eminent positions. " Je meurs de faim," he wrote in the letter which accompanied every copy; " depuis quinze jours je mange du pain et je bois de l'eau, je travaille sans feu, et j'ai vendu jusqu'à mes habits pour fournir aux frais de copies de mon travail." Cuvier alone encouraged him to proceed; the work in his opinion contained some new and important ideas.[17] The ' Introduction aux Travaux Scientifiques,' which was written in 1808, will be chiefly remembered in literature as the earliest work in which the words "philosophie positive " occur.[18] There has been considerable dispute on the part of M. Comte's disciples, as to the meaning Saint-Simon intended to convey by them; yet in the ' Science de l'Homme ' they are sufficiently explained. Since the fifteenth century, we are told, there has been a constant tendency in science to found all reasoning upon observed facts, in marked contrast to the previous method, in which imagination occupied a prominent place. Already the sciences of astronomy, physics, and chemistry have been placed upon this "base positive." Now particular sciences are the elements of general science, and general science is

---

[17] Hubbard, p. 59.

[18] The words are, " Avec quelle sagacité Descartes a dirigé ses recherches ! Il a senti que la philosophie positive se divisait en deux parties également importantes : la physique des corps bruts et la physique des corps organisés."—*Œuvres Choisies*, vol. i. p. 198.

philosophy. Philosophy must therefore have necessarily been conjectural so long as the particular sciences were conjectural, and demi-conjectural so long as some sciences were conjectural and some positive. There will therefore be a "philosophie positive," so soon as all the particular sciences have become positive. Now this has actually occurred with one exception, that of physiology; and in consequence of the peculiar complexity of the phenomena presented by man, there are some that cannot yet be accounted for upon strictly scientific principles; and hence there is still room for metaphysicians and moralists to indulge their imagination, precisely as astrologists and alchemists were accustomed to do in the infancy of astronomy and chemistry.[19] It follows that the great work that re-

---

[19] "On voit que la tendance de l'esprit humain depuis le xve siècle est de baser tous ses raisonnements sur des faits observés et discutés; que déjà il a réorganisé sur cette base positive l'astronomie, la physique, la chimie. . . . On voit que les sciences particulières sont les éléments de la science générale; que la science générale, c'est-à-dire la philosophie, a dû être conjecturale tant que les sciences particulières l'ont été; qu'elle a dû être mi-conjecturale et positive quand une partie des sciences particulières est devenue positive, pendant que l'autre était encore conjecturale, et qu'elle sera tout-à-fait positive quand toutes les sciences particulières le seront: ce qui arrivera à l'époque où la physiologie et la psychologie seront basées sur des faits observés et discutés."—*Œuvres Choisies*, vol. ii. pp. 14, 15. Elsewhere ('Œuvres,' vol. xvii. p. 109) he says, "En examinant le caractère relatif et positif du tout et des parties de la science, on trouve que le tout et les parties ont dû commencer par avoir le caractère conjectural; qu'ensuite le tout et les parties ont dû avoir le caractère mi-conjectural et positif; qu'enfin le tout et les parties doivent acquérir autant que possible le caractère positif. Nous en sommes au point que le premier bon résumé des sciences particulières consti-

1813.

mains for this age to accomplish is to rescue physiology
from its conjectural condition, and this not so much
out of regard for the science itself, as because of the
intellectual revolution that it will produce; for the
transition will be then definitely effected from Deism to
Physicism, from the system of ideas that ascribes phenomena to the direct action of a divine will, instead of
to the natural operation of an invariable law.[20] Now
among the numerous errors embodied in proverbs,
there is none more absurd than that which ascribes a
great effect to an insignificant cause.   Europe is just
now passing through a severe political crisis, and a
little consideration will show that it is produced by
a cause of commensurate magnitude.   In truth, nothing can so powerfully agitate society as the dissolution of its general beliefs, nor can we expect that
social order will be restored till they have been re-
organized.   The transition from Polytheism to Deism
occurred amid the convulsions of an expiring empire;
and it cannot be strange that the struggle between
Physicism and Deism should be accompanied in our

tuera la philosophie positive.   Il a été jusqu'à présent impossible de
faire un bon système de philosophie; il est possible aujourd'hui de
réussir dans cette entreprise, mais cela n'est pas aisé, cela est même
fort difficile."   This was written in 1811.

[20] " Le système général de nos connaissances sera réorganisé ; son organisation sera basée sur la croyance que l'univers est régi par une seule
loi immuable.   Tous les systèmes religieux de politique, de morale, de
législation civile, seront mis en accord avec le nouveau système de nos
connaissances."— *Œuvres Choisies*, vol. ii. p. 183.

own day by a corresponding anarchy. The triumph of Physicism will effect the restoration of social order, and it may be even predicted that a great improvement in the theory of morals will accompany the advance to scientific religion. Such an improvement has always characterized each preceding development, and as the moral teaching of Christianity was infinitely superior to any the world had ever seen before, so we may hope the new religion will surpass its predecessors.

It is therefore to the great task of raising physiology to the rank of a positive science, that Saint-Simon directs the attention of his contemporaries. The materials have nearly all been collected by Vicq-d'Azyr, Cabanis, Bichat, and Condorcet; it remains merely to generalize the results of their investigations, and the science of man will be formed. The purely scientific portion has been already undertaken by M. Burdin. The labours of Saint-Simon will be chiefly directed to show that social and moral phenomena are due exclusively to certain physiological causes, and may therefore be justly regarded as a portion of the science of physiology. He therefore proceeds to argue that it is quite a mistake to imagine that there is any difference whatever between man and other animals, in consequence of any superior intelligence or soul that belong to the former. These are to be attributed solely to physical organization, and are perfect in proportion to its perfection. At first Saint-Simon feared that the monkey might furnish a contradiction to this theory, for though it is not the most intelligent animal after man, it has been considered to be the next most perfect in its physical organization. But M. Burgon explained to him that this is an error due to theology.[21] The Bible has stated that man was made in the image of God, and naturalists have therefore considered that there must be some inherent perfection in his peculiar upright form. This, however, is by no means the case, for it may be proved that the beaver is physically the next most perfect creature; it happens that it is also precisely the most intelligent. Now, it is evident there is no reason whatever why the animal next in order in creation should not attain to the same perfection as man, provided the tyranny of his dominion be swept from the earth. If, therefore, this calamity should occur, the beaver will no doubt supply his place, it will follow the track of his development through the ages, and advance to intellect and high destiny as he has advanced.

Having removed this preliminary difficulty, Saint-Simon proceeds to show, by an elaborate appeal to history, that civilization is the result of a long series of progressive evolutions, the earliest being due exclusively to the slight physical superiority of man, and

---

[21] " L'intelligence de chaque animal est proportionnée à son organisation, par conséquent elle en est une conséquence, un effet: et l'échelle intellectuelle est la même que l'échelle organique."—*Œuvres Choisies*, vol. ii. p. 38.

1813.   each successive step being the necessary result of its immediate predecessor.

According to this theory, progress must have been continual—retrogression impossible. How then could the middle ages have been, as commonly represented, inferior to those that preceded them? This difficulty was solved by M. Ælsner. He explained that though the people still continued in the direction given by Socrates, the introduction of Arabian literature directed the attention of philosophers to the laws of nature, which prepared the way for the subsequent elimination of an Animated Cause. This is sufficient to show that the middle ages were not dark, but that even then the human mind was preparing to enter into the new phase of thought that has now culminated in Physicism.

The composition of the ' Science de l'Homme' occupied but fifteen days; a few months afterwards it was followed by an Essay on Gravitation, which purported to be an instalment of the great work already projected. It was dedicated to Napoleon Bonaparte, by Henry de Saint-Simon, cousin of the Duc de Saint-Simon, author of the ' Mémoires sur la Régence,' under the strange title, ' Moyen de forcer les Anglais à reconnaître l'Indépendance des Pavillons.' It is also called ' Travail sur la Gravitation Universelle,' because gravitation is destined to form the basis of the new philosophical theory, upon which every political structure will henceforth rest. The other title, which was more especially adapted to attract the attention of the Emperor, is also quite appropriate, inasmuch as it is certain that it will form a part of the new political system to force the English to recognise the independence of maritime flags; but it will not the less induce Bonaparte to renounce the protectorate of the Rhine, to grant freedom to Holland, and to withdraw from interference in the affairs of Spain. In this work Saint-Simon brings into still clearer relief the main features of his doctrine. He endeavours to show that (1) recent discoveries in science have dissolved the belief in Deism, and therefore the spiritual power of the religion that was founded upon it.[22] (2.) That to this cause must be ascribed the existing anarchy in European society, not only in opinion but also in politics.[23] (3.) That reorganization is the special mission of the present century.[24] (4.) That no reorganization can be effected, except it be based upon the general system of ideas derived from the philo-

[22] "Il y avait déjà quinze cents ans que cette théorie était organisée; il n'était pas étonnant qu'elle se trouvât insuffisante pour disposer dans le meilleur ordre les connaissances que l'esprit humain possédait quinze cents ans après, et il était impossible qu'elle pût lier les faits qui n'avaient été découverts que postérieurement à son établissement."— *Œuvres Choisies,* vol. ii. p. 189.

[23] "La crise dans laquelle toute la population européenne se trouve engagée, n'a d'autre cause que l'incohérence des idées générales.—*Ib.* p. 241.

[24] "Réorganiser la société européenne, seul objet philosophique qui mérite de fixer l'attention des savants dans ce moment."—*Ib.* p. 242.

1818. sophy of science.[25] (5.) That the principle of gravitation will be the foundation of that system.[26] (6.) That a religion will arise, based upon science, with a priesthood selected from among those who are proficient in positive knowledge.[27] (7.) That these will establish a spiritual power equal to that formerly possessed by Christianity, and will supersede it. (8.) And in this manner society will be once more relieved from anarchy and the ambition of kings and peoples restrained.[28]

We have already seen that the middle ages were not in the opinion of Saint-Simon a period of retrogression, because it was then that Arabian science found its way into Europe, and those studies were begun which have subsequently contributed so powerfully to the progress of mankind. But in his memoir on Gravitation he has propounded another reason—

[25] "Vous avez bien raison de prêcher qu'il faut une théorie générale et que c'est seulement sous son rapport philosophique que la science est directement utile à la société ; et que les savants peuvent former la corporation politique générale qui est nécessaire pour lier entre elles les nations européennes et pour mettre un frein à l'ambition des peuples et des rois."—Œuvres Choisies, p. 238.

[26] "Cette philosophie sera certainement basée sur l'idée de la GRAVITATION UNIVERSELLE, et tous vos travaux prendront, dès ce moment, un caractère systématique."

[27] "Le pouvoir spirituel passera dans les mains d'un pape et d'un clergé physicistes."—Ib. p. 244.

[28] "Aussitôt qu'il y aura une théorie proportionnée à l'état des lumières, tout rentrera dans l'ordre. L'institution commune des peuples européens se rétablira d'elle-même, et un clergé d'une instruction proportionnée aux connaissances acquises rétablira promptement le calme en Europe en mettant un frein à l'ambition des peuples et des rois."—Ib. p. 241.

that the real claim of the middle ages to superiority   .1813.
over any preceding epoch in history is the separation
which was then for the first time effected between the
spiritual and temporal powers. "The only point," he
writes, "upon which modern historians are agreed is an
error. They have all agreed to call the ages between
the ninth and the fifteenth centuries ages of barbarism,
while, in truth, it was then that the institutions were
formed which now give to European society its dis-
tinctive superiority. Let us see what were the political institutions of that period. The first that presents
itself to the mind is the division between the spiritual
power and the temporal power; this division is so admirable that it admits of no further improvement."[29]

History, he adds, has been called the breviary of
kings. It is clear, however, from their conduct either
that they do not study their breviary to profit, or else
that the breviary is itself valueless. History, in truth,
is still in its infancy as a science: it consists at present of a collection of facts more or less authentic, but
they have never yet been collected together by any
scientific theory; they have never yet been viewed as
links in one vast chain of sequences. Thus history is
unable to fulfil any of the functions of a science; it
has been a record of the past, but it can be no guide
to the future. Historians have been more occupied in
detailing the actions of individuals than in tracing the

[29] 'Œuvres Choisies,' vol. ii. p. 197.

progress of the race. Their attention has been directed
to particular incidents, but not to the general laws
that govern them; hence they are unable to act as
the counsellors of kings by propounding the principles
that should regulate political action.

In the course of the work of which the essay on
gravitation is a part, Saint-Simon will trace the past,
future, and present of the human race in the order
named. The vast deserts of Asia and Africa supply
the key to the history of the final destiny of mankind;
for the whole surface of the globe is advancing
through slow stages to the same condition. Man will
gradually be exterminated from the face of the earth
by its becoming an arid waste. An attempt will be
made to depict the feelings of the only remnant of
humanity, when, having drunk the last drop of water
in the world, he lies down to die; his death struggle will
indeed be greater than any that have ever yet afflicted
the sons of men, for, besides his own, he will have to
bear the agonies of an expiring race. But it is not to
be supposed that humanity will retain, to this disastrous close of its brilliant career, those high faculties
which are now its pride. On the contrary, when it per-
ceives the inevitable destiny reserved for it, it will then
rapidly deteriorate until it returns to the low condition
from which it sprang, until, in fact, man becomes animated by no higher desires than the animal, whose condition he originally so nearly resembled. It is pleasant

to turn from this gloomy picture to the contemplation   1814.
of a period of unexampled splendour which man is previously destined to traverse, when the mind shall have
been freed from every superstition that clouds it, and
when the system of the Universe shall have been displayed by the perfection of science.

Saint-Simon had not, as yet, gained any literary
reputation. His 'Letters from Geneva' had attracted
very little attention, and were now completely forgotten; since then he had published nothing. Some of his
tracts remained in manuscript, others were printed,
but in neither case were they offered for sale; and he
was known, therefore, to only a limited circle of eminent persons to whom he sent copies of his writings.
His essay on Gravitation was brought under the notice
of the Emperor, and submitted to the Institute, but the
result was not favourable to the author. Napoleon
expressed his conviction that Saint-Simon was simply
a fool; the time had, however, arrived when, fool or no
fool, he was about to take a position among the theorists
of the age. Augustin Thierry, then about nineteen
years of age, joined him as pupil and literary assistant,
and they went to live in an apartment opposite the École
Normale. In October, 1814, they published an essay
'Concerning the Reorganization of European Society,
or the means of uniting the various nations of Europe
into the political body, and at the same time pre-
serving the national independence of each.'

D 2

1814. During the Middle Ages, it asserted, there existed a Supreme Court of Appeal at Rome, to which international disputes could be referred. The decline of Catholicism has deprived Europe of the advantages of that tribunal, and the essay before us proposes to establish a successor, adapted to the changed conditions of society. It is accordingly suggested that a king be chosen as a royal pope, to be the king of kings; the mode of his election will be explained upon another occasion. The dignity will be hereditary, and he will be established in an independent city. Inasmuch as it is capable of scientific demonstration that Parliamentary government is the best attainable—the king of kings will be a constitutional monarch, assisted by a House of Peers or a House of Commons; this latter will be composed of commercial men, the learned classes, magistrates, and administrators. Every million of men who can read and write will elect one representative of each of these classes; there will be a new election every ten years. The candidate must possess property in land to the amount of £1000 a year. But in order that an alliance may be cemented between property and talent, without which society can never be solidly established, it is proposed that, at each election, twenty persons shall be chosen, irrespective of property, from among those who are most highly distinguished for ability; the Government will then confer upon them the necessary property qualification. The

House of Peers will consist of gentlemen possessing £20,000 a year in land; their peerage will be here-ditary. Twenty of their number will be chosen from among the men who, by their labours in science and industry, have rendered the most eminent services to society. Thus will be constructed a Parliament of men, a federation of the world. The duties of this dis-tinguished assembly will be to arrange, without re-course to war, all the differences that may arise between nation and nation. It will also direct works of great public utility; it will connect the Danube with the Rhine, and the Rhine with the Baltic. It will regulate the education of Europe, and supply a code of public morality; it will likewise endeavour to spread the European race over the whole habitable globe. It is obvious that such a Parliament as this cannot be esta-blished until each country has individually adopted the parliamentary system; this, however, will no doubt be gradually accomplished. The manifest advantages it affords will be a sufficient inducement; but an alliance between France and England will materially hasten the event. These two countries have already adopted that system, and are, therefore, the fit pro-pagandists of their political faith. Let there be, there-fore, an Anglo-French Parliament, giving the propor-tion to the English in the relation of two to one—inas-much as that nation is most accustomed to Parliamen-tary government, and has, also, least to gain by the

1814. alliance. Such an arrangement will be to their mutual
advantage, and will give them so great a power, that
their united efforts will be sufficient to reorganize the
whole of Europe. Without such a government, England will not be able to support the burden of her debt,
nor will France be able to retain her constitutional
government. The alliance will preserve the one nation
from bankruptcy, and the other from revolution. England will give stability to the French Government, and
France will gratefully share England's debt; she will
feel that it was a debt contracted in an heroic effort to
preserve a refuge for liberty in Europe, in which liberty
she herself now participates. In conclusion, Saint-
Simon prophesies that "a time will undoubtedly come
when all the nations of Europe will feel that questions
of general interest should predominate over those that
are merely national. The misery with which society is
now oppressed will then diminish, the troubles with
which its peace is now menaced will disappear; wars
will cease. The inspiration of poets has placed the
golden age at the cradle of humanity, amid the ignorance and barbarity of early times; it had been better
to relegate the iron age to that period. The golden
age of the human race is not behind, but before us, it
lies in the perfectibility of society. Our fathers have
not seen it, it is reserved for our children to behold it;
it is for us to make ready the way."

Saint-Simon possessed the art, which during periods

of revolution is peculiarly useful, of adapting his
opinions according to the requirements of the moment.
When the revolution broke out, he hastened to throw
aside his titles of nobility, and he flattered the passions
of the mob by violent speeches; at the same time, he
took advantage of unjust confiscations to accumulate a
large personal fortune, which he fancied would afterwards enable him to apply his great talents to the benefit of mankind.   So long as Napoleon's fortunes were
in the ascendant, no sycophant was ever more obse-
quious.   The Emperor was not merely the political
chief, but also the scientific chief, of humanity; in one
hand he held the "Infaillible Compas," in the other,
the exterminating sword, raised against all opponents
of enlightenment.   The most illustrious scholars should
assemble round his throne, not less than the most
valiant captains.   Saint-Simon, in his capacity of
scholar, was very well inclined to adopt his own advice.
He addressed his writings to the Emperor, he impor-
tuned help from him, he even inquired from the Baron
de Gerando what form it would be expedient to give
to his works in order to please Napoleon.[30]   No sooner,
however, had the Emperor retired to Elba, than all this
was changed.   He had terrified Europe by a mad project of universal dominion; nothing could be more
antagonistic to the spirit of the age, nothing could
more effectually retard the progressive advance of

[30] 'Œuvres,' vol. xvii. p. 141.

1815. society than a recurrence to military despotism. Every year the interests of France were more completely sacrificed to unprincipled ambition. In a small tract entitled 'Profession of Faith of the Comte de Saint-Simon respecting the Invasion of French Territory by Napoleon Bonaparte,' he prophesies that Napoleon and his family must always be tyrants. "A man appears on our frontiers," he adds, "who, during ten years, has desolated France by the excess of military despotism."

Having hastily abandoned the declining fortunes of the great emperor, it was of course necessary to look elsewhere for patronage and assistance; he accordingly applied to bankers and persons engaged in industrial pursuits. His subsequent writings were published by subscription; but MM. Lafitte and Ternaux were his principal supporters. This change of circumstances determined also a corresponding modification of opinion. The reader may have perhaps remarked the immense importance Saint-Simon attached to the possession of territorial property; his earliest work indeed enforces the moral obligation of labour, and he shows throughout a very high esteem for learning, whether literary or scientific, but industrial pursuits seem barely to have attracted his attention. It was time now to repair this mistake; he therefore pointed out that there are many reasons in favour of transferring political power from the hands of the territorial

proprietors to those of the industrial classes. In the
first place, industry suffers more than land from the
effects of violence, and therefore manufacturers have a
more personal interest in the preservation of order.
Besides this, their intelligence is greater, for their intellects have been stimulated by exertion: the habits
of business they have acquired will be most profitable
when applied to the service of the State, and the intimate relation in which they stand to the poor points to
them as the natural legislators for the people. Indeed
society should be comprised exclusively of two classes,
the learned and the industrial; the one engaged in
investigating the laws of nature, the other in pro-
ducing by the application of those laws what is useful
and agreeable. In other words, the whole of mankind
should be engaged in industry, theoretical or practical.
It will be perceived that no room is left in this division for those who live in idleness upon the property
they have inherited.[31] In order to expound these
opinions, he commenced the publication of 'L'Industrie' in 1816; the work was not completed till 1818.
He adopted the motto—

> " Tout par l'Industrie,
> Tout pour l'Industrie."

He was assisted by various collaborators, among others,

[31] " Les nobles, les propriétaires de terres, non-cultivateurs . . . ce
que nous proposons serait un coup mortel pour eux." He condemns
" le régime gouvernemental, dans lequel les travailleurs se trouvent
sous la direction des désœuvrés."—Hubbard, pp. 207–209.

by Augustin Thierry, Saint-Aubin, Chaptal, and by
Auguste Comte. Charles Comte, who then wrote in
the 'Censeur,' had observed that society could only be
organized for production or for robbery; the latter
was the military *régime*, the former will be the industrial.[32] Improving upon this maxim, Saint-Simon
added that it was equally applicable to individuals;
in other words, those who are not directly engaged in
production, as they are nevertheless consumers, must
of necessity obtain their means of livelihood by robbery.[33] There are, however, two exceptions, those
classes who are employed to protect the property that
has been produced, and those who are engaged in
philosophical meditation upon political questions. The
robbers are a large and formidable body; it includes
proprietors of land, fundholders, and mendicants.
This classification is perhaps a little startling, but it
has been accepted by many who are not disciples of
Saint-Simon.

[32] "Une nation doit nécessairement s'organiser pour un de ces deux
buts, celui de *voler* ou celui de *produire*, c'est-a-dire qu'elle doit avoir
le *caractère industriel*, sous peine de n'être qu'une *association bâtarde*,
si elle ne se prononce pas franchement dans l'un de ces deux sens."—
Œuvres, vol. xix. p. 157.

[33] "Il y a autour de la société . . . une foule d'hommes parasites—
qui, ne produisant rien, consomment ou veulent consommer comme s'ils
produisaient. Il est de force que ces gens-là vivent sur le travail
d'autrui, soit qu'on leur donne, soit qu'ils prennent; en un mot, il y a des
fainéants, c'est-à-dire des voleurs. Les fainéants qui ne sont point voleurs
se font mendiants : cette dernière classe n'est guère moins méprisable et
moins dangereuse que la première."—*Œuvres*, vol. xviii. p. 130.

Now it is in order to protect society from the depre-
dations of these "*hommes parasites*," these "*désœuvrés*,"
these "*fainéants*," these "*consommateurs*," that it is
necessary to have a government armed with power.[34]
This government should be extremely cheap, and entirely in the hands of the industrial classes, amongst
whom he includes agriculturists. But in order that the
latter may assume their true position, it will be necessary to alter the relation in which they at present stand
to their landlords. In other branches of industry the
person who undertakes a business occupies an independent position, but in agriculture the farmer is dependent
upon his sleeping partner, *i.e.* his landlord, whom he
even calls master. The land is a portion of the capital
of the cultivator; unlike the manufacturer, however,
this capital is placed under the most vexatious restric-
tions. The farmer is obliged upon all occasions to apply
to his landlord for permission to make any improvement
or alteration; this inconvenience should be remedied
by a measure of Tenant Right. An estimate of the
value of a farm should be taken at the commencement
and at the expiration of every lease. The landlord should
be compelled to lend the farmer whatever amount of

[34] " Les travailleurs sont donc exposés à se voir privés de la jouis-
sance qui est le but de leur travail. De ce danger résulte pour eux un
besoin d'une espèce particulière, lequel donne lieu à un travail distinct
des autres, celui qui a pour but d'empêcher la violence dont l'oisiveté
menace l'industrie. Aux yeux de l'industrie, un gouvernement n'est
autre chose que l'entreprise de ce travail."—*Œuvres*, vol. xviii. p. 130.

money he may require for the improvement of the property; and its employment should be confided entirely to the judgment of the tenant. If the farm has
increased in value during the tenancy, then the landlord will share in the improvement; if the value has
diminished, he will likewise participate in the loss.
All cases of dispute to be referred to arbitration.
Still further to increase the facilities for improvement,
"*banques territoriales*" will spring up, with the view
to afford the same advantages to agriculturists that
are now enjoyed by manufacturers. The political
franchise has been hitherto confided to the proprietor,
but it should in future be transferred to the occupier,
who will, as a consequence, pay the public burdens.
Under the new system of industrialism, however, taxes
will be vastly reduced. As society is at present constituted, the governing classes have a direct interest
to increase them, for as they fill all public functions,
they alone profit by them; but when power has been
consolidated in the hands of industrials, this will be
no longer the case. Lawyers also are, as a body, es-
sentially obstructive; they adhere with tenacity to
traditions that have become obsolete, and resist every
measure of reform; they are, too, as we have seen,
robbers, for they produce nothing, and therefore are
driven either to extortion or to beggary. While we
fully recognize that at a former period they rendered
substantial service to society by delivering it from

even worse evils, yet we cannot fail to see the neces- sity of abolishing them now.[35] Their functions will be undertaken by unpaid courts of arbitration, composed exclusively of the industrial classes, who have never had their natural sense of justice perverted by a study of law; such is the new organization to which Saint-Simon believes society to be tending. Stated briefly, he holds that the position of agriculturists will be assimilated to that of the manufacturer, the two together forming an industrial community, in whose hands all the power at present exercised by the government and the legal profession will centre. This new organization will be known as the industrial *régime*, and will form a very striking contrast to the military and feudal *régime*, out of which we are emerging. The present is a period of transition, and consequently of disturbance; it may be known by the dissolution of the general principles that have guided human conduct since the establishment of Deism amid similar convulsions, and the absence as yet of any new principles to supply the place of the old. " The human mind," he says, " has advanced since the establishment of Christian mo-

---

[35] " Cette institution [courts of law] peut et doit être remplacée dans toutes ses parties par des tribunaux industriels, qui ne sont autre chose que des arbitrages, seule jurisprudence nécessaire quand il n'existera plus d'autres propriétés que des propriétés industrielles." "Toutes les affaires peuvent et doivent être jugées arbitralement, même les affaires criminelles, qui en paraissent le moins susceptibles."—Quoted by Hubbard, pp. 181, 189.

rality, and as a result of its progress, the era of theology has passed by, never to return; it would be
madness to attempt to found a system of morals upon
a belief in the supernatural, which is now generally
ridiculed.   Christianity has contributed much to
morals,—it would be unjust to deny it,—but its reign
has ended, its utility has long since ceased; the era
of positive ideas begins. We can no longer give to
morality other sanctions but palpable, certain, and
present interest; such is the spirit of this age, such
it will continue to be for all future generations. The
great step which civilization is about to accomplish
will consist in the establishment of a system of terrestrial and positive morality."[36] Measures should therefore be taken as speedily as possible to influence public
opinion in this direction by the teaching of a more
instructed clergy. A law should be passed without
delay to prohibit the ordination of a priest until he
has proved by public examination that he is familiar
with the principal results of the positive sciences; that
is to say, he must exhibit a knowledge of pure and
applied mathematics, of physics, of chemistry, and
of physiology.[37] Until by this means we once more
regain a definite system of general principles, our conduct will continue to be inconsistent, and the condition
of society anarchical.[38] We shall be misled by a senti-

[36] 'Œuvres,' vol. xix. p. 38.   [37] Ib, vol. xix. p. 41.
[38] " C'est le défaut d'idées générales qui nous a perdus, nous ne renaî-

ment, instead of guided by a principle. We shall
struggle for nationality, for equality, for military
glory,[39] we shall endeavour to make a compromise with
the past and the future, and to erect it into a body of
doctrine under the name of Conservatism, or station-
aryism,[40] and to embody it in a political system, such
as, for instance, parliamentary government.[41] But
when the transition in philosophy from theological to
positive morals has been accomplished, the corresponding transition in politics from the military or
predatory *régime* to the industrial *régime* will speedily
follow.[42] The general principle of *terrestrial* utility derived from morals will be applied to politics, which

1816
to
1818.

trons véritablement que par des idées générales ; les anciennes sont
tombées de vétusté et ne peuvent se rajeunir, il nous en faut de nouvelles."—*Œuvres*, vol. xviii. p. 213.

[39] "Au défaut d'idées communes, on se rallia à des sentiments généraux. Les passions nationales se créèrent, l'égalité et la gloire militaire
enivrèrent tour à tour les esprits, et le despotisme trouva bientôt sa
place."—*Ib.* p. 207.

[40] "Les gens que j'appelle stationnaires sont ceux qui, se parant mal
à propos du titre de raisonnables, veulent amalgamer au nom de la
modération les institutions anciennes avec les nouvelles, ils ne s'aper-
çoivent pas que c'est une entreprise absurde, que de tenter la fusion de
ces contraires."—*Ib.* vol. xviii. p. 169.

[41] "En nous laissant aller en étourdis au même enthousiasme, à cette
admiration irréfléchie qui ne laisse rien supposer au-delà de la constitution anglaise, peut-être allons-nous encore nous donner des entraves."—
Ib. vol. xix. p. 79. Cf. p. 27.

[42] "La transition qui s'opère actuellement se compose . . . de deux
autres : l'une philosophique, l'autre politique. La première consiste
dans le passage du système théologique au système terrestre et positif ;
la seconde, dans le passage du régime arbitraire au régime libéral et
industriel."—*Ib.* p. 25.

will then organize society solely with a view to produce the greatest possible amount at the least possible
cost.[43] Politics, in short, will become the science of
production ;[44] for it is not the mere form of government that is the question of the greatest importance
or difficulty in politics, but it is " to ascertain in what
manner property should be constituted so as to produce
the greatest benefit to society in general, both as
regards liberty and riches."[45]

The 'Industrie' was the last work of Saint-Simon
to which Thierry contributed, and it was the first in
which he received the assistance of Auguste Comte,
his young pupil. Comte was born at Montpellier,
in 1798, and he joined Saint-Simon in 1816. He
continued for six years to have relations with him
in the capacity of pupil, literary assistant, and
friend. Saint-Simon's own resources were by far too
precarious to render this connection advantageous pe-
cuniarily. It does not appear that more than one
quarter's salary was ever paid; and Comte already
supported himself, as he continued to do through
a great part of his life, by teaching mathematics.
At first his relations with Saint-Simon were pecu-

[43] " Que la production des choses utiles est le seul but raisonnable et
positif que les sociétés politiques puissent se proposer."—*Œuvres*, vol.
xviii. p. 186.

[44] " La politique est donc, pour me résumer en deux mots, *la science
de la production*, c'est-à-dire la science qui a pour objet l'ordre de choses
le plus favorable à tous les genres de productions."—*Ib.* p. 188.

[45] *Ib.* vol. xix. p. 83.

liarly friendly, and considerable advantage to both was the result; unhappily they parted in anger, and their respective disciples have seen fit to perpetuate the quarrel. Comte does not appear to have supplied any original matter to the 'Industrie,' but the third volume was intrusted to him to edit. The first essay we have from his pen relates to the 'Séparation générale entre les Opinions et les Désirs;' it is referred to 1819, the year following the completion of the 'Industrie,' but it was not published till very many years afterwards, in the Appendix to the 'Politique Positive.' In it he points out how absurd it would be to attempt to decide upon a question in physical science without possessing the smallest knowledge of the subject; but in politics, which is a science of even greater complexity, no such hesitation appears. Following Saint-Simon, he ascribes this peculiarity to the want of unanimity among the "spiritual" classes; nor can harmony be established until such time as politics shall have been, like astronomy, placed upon a positive basis. Hence, again following Saint-Simon, he suggests that society should be divided into three classes, (1) the "spiritual," excluded from political offices, and engaged in the elaboration of scientific politics; (2) the "temporal," charged with the execution of the social projects supplied by the former; and (3) the people, to whom he assigns the privilege of declaring in what direction they desire their efforts to be employed,—leaving to the " spiritual " classes the duty of ascertaining how best their wishes can be carried into effect.

Saint-Simon's next work, 'Le Politique,' appeared in detached numbers at irregular intervals during the early part of the year 1819; it repeated the views which have been already stated, and advocated in addition the abandonment of the system of standing armies, which are opposed to industry. It explained that as manufactures are exposed to complete destruction by war, while land can only be temporarily affected by it, the owners of the former are naturally more disposed to peace, and therefore better qualified to be intrusted with political power; partly for this reason, and partly because their interest is identified with the reduction of taxes, they should have the exclusive privilege of a seat in the national representative assembly, from which all public functionaries should be rigorously excluded.

Saint-Simon commenced the publication of the 'Organisateur' in November, 1819, and perhaps we may already trace in it the influence of Comte. It consists of a series of fourteen letters, which appeared successively, and were intended to remedy an error into which the author had fallen in the ' Industrie ' and repeated with further exaggeration in the 'Politique.' In these works he had injudiciously given to industry a predominance of authority which should be enjoyed only by learning. It is now sufficiently recognized that 1819
to
1820. government exists for the good of society, but great confusion still remains as to the nature of that good. There is, therefore, no uniformity of aim among the nations of Europe: one sovereign attempts to compass the good of his people by indulging his lust for conquest, another by the erection of public monuments, or the magnificence of his court, while another, differently inspired, may even endeavour to "organize his subjects for heaven." It is necessary, therefore, that the people themselves should decide wherein consists their own good, and that then they should not suffer themselves to be turned aside from its pursuit by any idiosyncrasy on the part of their rulers. It is clear, however, that the learned classes are alone competent to ascertain in what consists the good of society; for it is a subject that admits of strictly scientific investigation. The decision arrived at will command universal assent, because, being the result of scientific demonstration, it will be as incontestable as any other judgment established by scientific inquiry. Every one will not indeed be able to follow the course of reasoning by which the solution will be reached; but it will not the less be entitled to acceptance. Few men can demonstrate the revolution of the earth round the sun, but it is not the less certainly believed upon the faith of those who can, and in the same manner when the learned have

1819.
to
1820.

come to a unanimous solution of the various problems of society by a purely scientific process, their decision will likewise command the respect of the ignorant. Now, Saint-Simon considers that the good of society is attained by the satisfaction of its physical and moral wants; and that the object of government is to apply knowledge and wealth to that end. He therefore proposed the formation of an industrial parliament, to consist of three chambers,—the chambers of invention, of examination, of execution; the first, to be composed of 300 members, civil engineers, poets, scholars, sculptors, architects and musicians. The civil engineers, however, will predominate, they will number 200. The object of this chamber will be to project public works, and to increase the riches of France. The second chamber will consist likewise of 300 members, of whom 100 will be mathematicians, 100 professors of mathematical physics, and 100 physicians. These persons will examine and comment on the proceedings of the first chamber; they will adopt a plan of secular education, and will superintend its operation. The members of these two chambers will each receive a salary of 10,000 francs. The third chamber will be composed of the leaders of industry; they will be unpaid. They will be charged with executing the measures approved by the two higher assemblies; they will conduct the executive government, and vote the taxes. In this manner

a great anomaly will be removed from society, for " the
existing social organization is in fact the world turned
upside down, inasmuch as those who are the most
useful to society, who improve its condition, and add
to its riches, occupy a subordinate position to persons
who are totally useless, and often very expensive."
In order to impress this truth with greater vividness
upon the mind of the reader, Saint-Simon thought
fit to throw his ideas into the form of a parable. In it
he enumerates many of the trades, professions, and other
occupations of life, and asks with some appearance
of truth, whether the principal persons employed in
those pursuits would not be a greater loss than any of
the members of the royal family, or than any of the ministers of state.   He unfortunately mentioned by name
several persons of eminence, and amongst others the
Duke of Berry.   The assassination of the Duke in the
following year, exposed Saint-Simon to a public pro-
secution,—he was accused of having incited to murder ; the charge, which was quite unfounded, ended
in an acquittal.   The trial brought Saint-Simon pro-
minently before the public, and afforded him an
opportunity of addressing four letters to the jury who
were to try him.   He professed his loyalty to the
Bourbon family, and admitted that they should occupy
the throne so long as royalty continued to exist in
France ; he, however, prophesied their fall, unless
they allied themselves with the people.

The first essay published by Comte, was contributed anonymously to the 'Organisateur' of April, 1820. In a "Sommaire Appréciation de l'ensemble du Passé moderne" he adopted most of what is important in the speculations of Saint-Simon, but he illustrated his argument with a degree of learning, and stated it with a precision peculiarly his own. Modern history, he says, exhibits a twofold movement,—in the region of speculation, a transition from Catholicism to Positivism; in the region of Politics, a transition from feudalism to industrialism. At the period of the complete establishment of the two former, the seed of their future destruction was sown. The introduction of scientific studies into the Arabian schools was the ultimate cause of the one, while the enfranchisement of the commons produced the other; the first determined Luther's reform, and the second . the rise of parliamentary government. But these opinions were not however new, as they had been previously propounded by Saint-Simon in the 'Industrie,' and some of them even earlier.

In 1821, the 'Système Industriel' was published; it is a reproduction of several pamphlets, which Saint-Simon had addressed to the king and to leading manufacturers during the last six months of the preceding year, and to which he added an "Adresse aux Philanthropes." Before the publication of this last work, Saint-Simon can hardly be included among the socialist

writers of Europe. He had repeatedly asserted, indeed,
that the ancient *régime* of feudalism had passed away ;
he had vehemently attacked the clergy and lawyers ;
he. had 'suggested that the legal system be abolished
and courts of arbitration substituted in its stead.   All
existing religions incurred his contempt; he proposed
to replace the ascendancy of the clergy by that of lay
scholars, who were, in his opinion, the true guides of
humanity.   But while he advocated these radical
changes in the constitution of society, the interest of
the people themselves occupied but little of his
attention.   He frequently denounced the violence into
which a democracy is ready to fall; the horrors of
the French revolution were never absent from his mind.
In the ' Lettres de Genève,' the problem to be solved
by government was stated to be how order should be
maintained among a starving people; this could only
be effected by their subjugation; an alliance was therefore suggested between intellect and territorial property.   At the same time he conceded to the learned
classes a power which was not inferior to that which
the clergy possessed during the middle ages; the one
was indeed suggested by the other, and intended to
supply its place.   In his parliament of nations, the
preponderance of power is transferred from the learned
to the wealthy.   No one can sit in the House of Peers
who has not £20,000 a year, in land, nor in the House
of Commons unless he has £1000 a year, also in land.

The twenty persons who are to be elected for their learning are even to receive the requisite property qualification. As Saint-Simon continued his speculations, he lost sight more and more of the claims of the learned classes; at the same time his later essays transfer the entire temporal power from the owners of land to its cultivators and to the proprietors of manufactories. These persons are henceforth to direct the State; they are to sit in the tribunals of justice. Labour is declared to be the highest duty of a citizen, and the claim of idlers to exercise authority over the workers is contemptuously repudiated. In the midst of all this, Saint-Simon at length begins to see that perhaps a conspiracy between intellect and property to keep down the people, may not be of all constitutions the best. He observes that too much attention has been directed to the mere political organization of society, and that the social condition of the people is of even greater importance; he lays down therefore that the object of government should be to extend the circle of well-being, so as to include the greatest posssible number. As this view acquires more clearness, it eventually leads him to Socialism. The bold ideas he had so frequently expressed, and the dangerous notoriety they had procured for their author, induced many of his industrial subscribers to withdraw their names from his list, and to repudiate any sympathy for his opinions. This circumstance may

have contributed, from what we already know of his 1821.
character, to modify his views as to the supreme merits
of the industrial classes, and to restore the learned
classes for a time to the position they had formerly
held in his estimation. Accordingly in the 'Organisateur' they are to occupy two chambers of the legis-
lature, while only the lowest is to be awarded to the
leaders of industry. The 'Système Industriel' carries
these views still further; its object is indicated by
the motto, "Dieu a dit, aimez-vous et secourez-vous
les uns les autres." The mission of society, it declares,
is to complete the work begun 1800 years ago by
Christianity: we have but to follow that example,
and to weave into the fabric of society the principles
of equality and brotherhood. The first step towards
the attainment of this great object is a measure of
general education; the largest item in the budget will
therefore be for public instruction. The second is to
abolish misery, by conceding to all the right to live;
accordingly the State will undertake to ensure labour
to all who have no other means of subsistence. This
measure of Socialism will be completed by the abolition
of titles of rank, and the recognition by public opinion
of the exclusive pre-eminence of learning and industry.
At the same time the Institute should be charged
with the composition of a new catechism, in accordance
with the present state of knowledge. Its teaching
would replace the old theologies, and nothing con-

trary to it would be permitted to be taught; nor would any one enjoy the right of citizen till he had passed an examination in it.[46]

Saint-Simon now lived in the Rue Richelieu, in the house once occupied by Molière. The small pension his family had granted him was deeply involved by the expense attending the publication of his various works. He applied to the public for a subscription, and hoped to be able himself to write the ' Catéchisme,' for the Institute showed no disposition to undertake it at his suggestion; but the power of accomplishing this task was not within his reach. He found himself once more reduced to the very verge of starvation; seeing no means of relief, nor any of furthering the great work of social reform for which alone he cared to live, he determined with his own hand to end the miseries of his life. Accordingly, having loaded a pistol, he decided to shoot himself when the hand of his watch pointed to a certain hour. In order, however, that his mind might remain in unimpaired serenity to the end, and that the triumph over superstition might be complete, he occupied the interval with reviewing the important schemes of social reform to which he had devoted his life. At length the appointed hour arrived, and he fired at himself, but the result was only a very severe wound in the face; he sought for assistance, but could find none, he therefore sat down upon his bed and

[46] ' Œuvres Choisies,' vol. iii. p. 46.

awaited the end with tranquillity. In this condition he
was found by Comte and Sarlardière, from whom he at
once inquired with philosophic composure for an explanation as to " how it is possible that a man can live
and think with seven slugs in his brain ; " but his
friends applied themselves to the relief of his wound
before they gratified his scientific curiosity.   For some
time it was doubtful whether he would live, and as
the pain was intense he begged that a vein might
be opened, so that his sufferings might terminate ; in
a few weeks, however, except for the loss of one of his
eyes, he had entirely recovered.

His efforts were at once directed to the composition
of the ' Catéchisme.' In it he reverts to a former phase
of opinion, and again restores the industrial classes to
the first position in society ; they are the *classe nour-
ricière,* and as everything is the result of industry everything should be subordinate to it.   No change in existing institutions can however be effected by violent
revolutions ; revolutions disintegrate society, and can
never organize it.   The only means to employ is the
influence of public opinion, which has been well called
the queen of the world.   It cannot be doubted that
society is inevitably tending towards the entire abolition of all institutions originating in feudalism, and the
substitution of those derived from industry.   Saint-
Simon is of opinion that France is nearer to this goal
than England, because in France the power of the

aristocracy has been gradually diminishing till it has become nearly extinct, whereas in England their power has, he says, constantly increased. It is only natural to expect that the aristocracy should be tenacious of their privileges, and that they will exercise all their influence to continue a state of society which favours them exclusively. Accordingly, in England the struggle will be more protracted, but its issue not less certain. The example of France will give an impulse which every country in Europe will feel. It was a great mistake to represent the parliamentary system of England as the best form of government that can be devised; it is, in fact, but a compromise between the two systems—the feudal and the industrial,—and as these must be necessarily antagonistic, the constitution of England, if indeed it merits that name, can only be transitory. During its existence, the country must always be in a state of crisis. France has suffered much from attempting to follow such an evil example. Among other misfortunes that at present afflict society is the deficient state of education, and the imperfect code of morals; it is therefore proposed to establish two colleges, one for the purpose of conducting scientific education, the other for the study of moral and political science. These colleges will be presided over by a third, which will be employed in co-ordinating the results arrived at by the other two. It will also draw up a code of laws in the interest of the majority, and regulate public instruction.

Auguste Comte was intrusted with the execution of
a portion of the Catechism, but he could not accomplish it to the satisfaction of his master, for they were
now separated by a fundamental difference of opinion.
Saint-Simon, who was perpetually changing his
opinions, at present maintained the pre-eminence of
industry over every other employment, and the possibility of reorganizing society upon a purely industrial
basis; while Comte held that the elaboration of the
science of politics must precede any attempt to change
the practical working of society. Two years before,
in 1822, Saint-Simon had printed 100 copies of a
pamphlet on the " Social Contract," to which Comte
had added a " Plan des Travaux Scientifiques néces-
saires pour réorganiser la Société." This essay contained opinions very strongly opposed to orthodox
theology, and therefore, from respect for the feelings
of his family, Comte published it under the name of
Saint-Simon. In the absence of any more suitable
paper, it was now republished with the new title of
' Système de Politique Positive ;' and the discussion
to which this proceeding gave rise was the immediate
cause of the rupture between the two authors. Comte
desired that his essay should now appear with his
name, and without what he considered to be the ridiculous description of ' Catéchisme des Industriels.'
Saint-Simon is said to have promised to comply with
both these requests, but to have broken the last, and

Comte had the mortification to find his "système" included in the 'Catéchisme;' it was, however, preceded by two prefaces, one by Saint-Simon and the other by Comte. Saint-Simon acknowledges that the work is very good from the point of view of its author, but that it does not exactly attain the object he had desired; it ascribes a preponderant *rôle* to generalities which were, in his opinion, of secondary importance. "Dans le système que nous avons conçu, la capacité industrielle est celle qui doit se trouver en première ligne." His pupil, on the contrary, views "la capacité aristoticienne comme la première de toutes, comme devant primer le spiritualisme, ainsi que la capacité industrielle et la capacité philosophique;" notwithstanding its imperfections, however, he declares that it is the best work that has ever appeared on the theory of politics. Comte, upon the other hand, is profuse in his compliments to Saint-Simon. "Ayant médité," he writes in his preface, "depuis longtemps les idées mères de M. Saint-Simon, je me suis exclusivement attaché à systématiser, à développer et à perfectionner la partie des aperçus de ce philosophe qui se rapporte à la direction scientifique. Ce travail a eu pour résultat la formation du système de politique positive que je commence aujourd'hui à soumettre au jugement des penseurs. J'ai cru devoir rendre publique la déclaration précédente, afin que, si mes travaux paraissent mériter quelque approbation, elle remonte au fondateur de l'école philosophique dont je m'honore de faire partie." At the very time Comte wrote these lines he addressed a letter to his friend and pupil, M. Gustave d'Eichthal, in which he bitterly complains of Saint-Simon.[47] He says that he had been warned not to trust a man whose morality was so low that the only object he sought was to make a noise in the world, and who did not care what means he took provided he succeeded. He adds that Saint-Simon fancies that he alone is able to find ideas, and that the ordinary laws of nature have been suspended in his favour, so that age has had no effect upon him; whereas, the best thing he can do is to retire from philosophical speculation for the future; such is his vanity, however, that no combination is possible with him, except on the part of an inferior intellect willing to act merely as his instrument. But so far as Comte is concerned, Saint-Simon is afraid of being eclipsed by him, and, therefore, he has sought to hide him from the public. In such angry words as these the connection that had lasted for six years was broken. Madame Comte has related to M. Littré that the affection between the master and the pupil was at first ardent and reciprocal; but as time went on, heated discussions arose, in which Saint-Simon displayed but little temper and M. Comte very little deference. In truth their position was one of great difficulty: upon

---

[47] The eulogistic preface was published in April, and the letter to M. d'Eichthal was written on the 1st of May.

one side there was the authority of age and the
assurance of vanity; upon the other, there was the
consciousness of far greater intellectual power, and an
inability to restrain the disputatious impetuosity of
youth.   It is only to be regretted that when the
passions excited at the moment had passed, M. Comte
did not recover his candour.   He continues at a much
later period to speak of his "funeste liaison avec un
jongleur dépravé," and to complain that their association had been for him "un malheur sans compen-
sation."

Some well-intentioned persons have accepted
M. Comte as a prophet, and have invested his
writings with an amount of sacredness, and his character with a degree of sanctity befitting the high
office they have claimed for him.   Their enthusiasm
merits some respect; for a few years ago, when
his works became known in this country, the party
of intolerance was more influential and noisy than
at present, and any one suspected of heresy was
certain to have been denounced as intellectually
contemptible and morally depraved.   It was natural, therefore, that those who had found in the
Positive Philosophy the solution of many perplex-
ing difficulties, and who saw in it the evidence of
the most intense and even heroic labour, should
resent the ignorant clamour which was raised against
its author.   In the contest that ensued, both

1824.

sides, as is usually the case, were led into excesses,
and it is natural that the zeal of the defenders should
increase till they altogether lost sight of the short-
comings of their hero, and vastly magnified his merits.
But there is no longer any necessity for such chivalrous devotion. No one who is of the smallest consequence would in these days be blind to the merits of a
philosopher because his opinions are not orthodox,
and it so happens that the most formidable opponents
of the infallibility of M. Comte are themselves suspected of that failing. It is time, therefore, to abandon the exaggerated tone which has been assumed
under the immediate pressure of defending a persecuted prophet. A careful inquiry will then perhaps
lead to the conviction that M. Comte is neither so
accurate, nor even so original as was at first supposed.
The accuracy of his views on physical science and
sociology have been contested by three of the ablest
writers in this country in their respective departments.[48]
I shall here only endeavour to indicate the numerous
points of similarity between the opinions, whether correct or false, that were advocated by Comte, and those
previously advocated by Saint-Simon. Now as Comte
passed six years of his life, between the ages of twenty

[48] Compare 'Auguste Comte and Positivism,' by J. S. Mill; second
edition; Trübner, 1866. 'Essays,' by Herbert Spencer, 2 vols.,
Williams and Norgate, 1868. 'Classification of the Sciences,' by Herbert Spencer; Williams and Norgate, 1869. 'Lay Sermons,' by T. H.
Huxley, F.R.S.; Macmillans, 1870.

F

and twenty-six, when the mind is the most susceptible to intellectual influences, in intimate association with Saint-Simon, it is only fair to conclude that this marked similarity is more than accidental, and that his life and opinions were in a great degree determined by that circumstance. M. Comte has yet much claim to our gratitude. There are no doubt many who have groped their way painfully and wearily through his long volumes, to find not perhaps in them, but in the line of thought they have suggested, a clue whereby they have been able to reconstruct for themselves a philosophy and system of morals, when the old landmarks have been removed. It is impossible to imagine that Saint-Simon could ever have done as much. Numerous as are the errors of M. Comte, those of Saint-Simon are immeasurably greater, and although the later writings of the former afford every opportunity for adverse and supercilious criticism, the writings of Saint-Simon are far more exposed to these attacks. There remains, however, sufficient to form a very distinct body of doctrine, and I shall endeavour, at the risk of wearying the reader by repetition, to show the point at which it had reached before 1818, when M. Comte, then twenty years of age, became acquainted with Saint-Simon.

I.

Saint-Simon had already maintained that from the earliest known epoch to the present hour, the human

race has continued to progress, that its advance has 1824.
been very gradual, and solely due to natural causes.
That at first, the imagination predominated largely over
the powers of observation,[49] and that knowledge was in
consequence for a long time mainly conjectural;[50] and
during this period, the phenomena of nature were referred to supernatural causes. The human mind has
passed through a series of theological stages, rising
from fetishism[51] to pure theism,—from the conception
that natural objects are severally gods, to the conception
that they are all submitted to the control of one God.[52]
The transition was determined by the growing power
of observation, by which a degree of regularity has been
displayed that can only be accounted for upon the
supposition of a single Divine will.[53] Philosophy had
attained to this condition so early as the time of Socrates,[54] but it was not embodied into a religion for
the people till much later, when it assumed the form
of Christianity.[55]

In the Arabian schools of the middle ages, the
faculty of observation was carried to still greater perfection,[56] and the labours then begun have been continued energetically to the present day. The result
has been to establish the absolute unvarying sequence
of phenomena so as to exclude the supposition of any

[49] See Appendix, No. 1.　　[50] Ib. No. 2.
[51] Saint-Simon generally used the word 'idolatry.' Fetishism was
not then in general use, but he meant by it substantially the same.
[52] See Appendix, No. 3.　[53] Ib. No. 4.　[54] Ib. No. 5.　[55] Ib. No. 6.
[56] Ib. No. 7.

1824. intervention whatsoever on the part of a supernatural
       Being.[57] The attention has been fixed with an ever-
       increasing interest upon the laws of Nature, and so
       far as science in its modern aspect is concerned with
       the existence of a God, it declares that the universe has
       been submitted to the control of laws from which, from
       the beginning, there has been no authenticated devia-
       tion.[58] Indeed, Saint-Simon went so far as to hold
       that the various laws of nature are subordinated to
       one general law, that of gravitation.[59] He considered
       that the transition from the conception of many su-
       pernatural causes, or polytheism, to one supernatural
       cause, or theism—is analogous to the transition, which
       he regarded as either impending or actually accom-
       plished, from the conception of many natural laws to
       that of one general law.[60]

       Such then, is the amazing contrast between the first
       and last conditions of human knowledge—between
       the Conjectural period, when all phenomena are held
       to be controlled by the will of one or many gods, and
       the Positive period, when they are submitted to the
       absolute reign of one or many natural laws.

       The movement gave rise to a long transitional
       period, during which some of the sciences remained
       in the conjectural or theological condition; while
       others had emerged, wholly or in part, into the posi-

       ---

       [57] See Appendix, No. 8.   [58] Ib. No. 9.   [59] Ib. No. 10.
                         [60] Ib. No. 11.

tive or scientific condition.[61] The reason of this is 1824.
sufficiently evident,—some phenomena are much less
complex and more easy of observation than others.
It is only natural to expect, therefore, that the sciences
of which they form the subject-matter should be the
first to discard supernaturalism ; and this is precisely
what history shows to have been the case.[62] The
sciences have followed one another in the order of
their simplicity; beginning with astronomy, passing
on to physics and chemistry, and ending with physiology.[63] At the time, indeed, when Saint-Simon
began to write, he complained that physiology was
still in many respects eminently conjectural.[64] In other
words, there remained a large portion of the phenomena of life, for which there had been discovered as
yet no sufficient scientific explanation, and which, as
a consequence, were still regarded by some as supernatural.[65] The moral nature of man and his political
condition were among the most difficult of these
problems. A highly unscientific and obstructive
class of persons had entrenched themselves behind
these extremely complex natural phenomena, concerning which they indulged in curious theological
and metaphysical speculations, and insisted with much
pertinacity, that here at least there was concealed a
sacred mystery, which the profane hands of science

[61] See Appendix, No. 12.   [62] Ib. No. 13.   [63] Ib. No. 14.
[64] Ib. No. 15.   [65] Ib. No. 16.

1824. could never unveil. It became, therefore, a matter of necessity to dislodge these persons, and Saint-Simon applied himself to the task. He proceeded, therefore, to show that mind and matter are but different forms of one substance ;[66] and that the whole of the superiority of man to the rest of the animal creation is to be ascribed to a very slight original difference of a purely physiological character.[67] From this starting-point, the whole of the phenomena of man and of society have been naturally evolved, and hence both morals and politics are positive sciences, and governed by laws which can be ascertained by experiment and observation — in a manner analogous to that pursued in astronomy or physics.[68]

II.

While the increasing faculty of observation has, in this manner, completely revolutionized science, science in its turn will revolutionize philosophy.[69] The knowledge we possess concerning the universe must necessarily affect the opinions we form concerning it.[70] To this circumstance are due the successive stages that have marked the progress from fetishism upwards, each stage being caused by a corresponding advance in our scientific knowledge.[71] "Religion," said Saint-Simon, meaning theology, "Religion is the popular.

[66] See Appendix, No. 17.   [67] Ib. No. 18.   [68] Ib. No. 19.
[69] Ib. No. 20.   [70] Ib. No. 21.   [71] Ib. No. 22.

language of science." Now it is clear that the tran-   1824.
sition which has been recently effected from Conjec-
turalism to Positivism, must determine a corresponding
transition from Deism to a philosophy which will supply a theory of the universe in accordance with the
present state of knowledge.[72] This was what Saint-
Simon sometimes called Physicism, sometimes Positive Philosophy.[73]

III.

Such, then, is the revolution that is now going
forward in opinion—from the supernatural interpreta-
tion of phenomena to the natural, from theology to
Positivism. But in politics an analogous movement
may be traced. Ever since the enfranchisement of the
Commons, the power of feudalism has continued to
decline, and that of industry to increase.[74] It is not
difficult, therefore, to perceive that, as in the one department the scientific classes will acquire 'spiritual'
power,—so, in the other, the industrial classes will be
invested with 'temporal' authority.[75] In order to conciliate the two extremes—feudalism and industrialism
—there arose a transitional period of Parliamentary
government. But the general ideas upon which it is
founded are purely negative, and it is, therefore, impossible that society can repose upon them, and hence
the organization of society upon the industrial system

[72] See Appendix, No. 23.   [73] Ib. No. 24.   [74] Ib. No. 25.
[75] Ib. No. 26.

is dependent upon the elaboration of a positive philosophy and politics.[76]

IV.

Saint-Simon maintained that the middle ages could not justly be considered to have been a period of retrogression, because it was then for the first time that the spiritual and temporal powers were completely separated,—an event to which he attached immense importance.[77] He ascribed the stability of society to the existence of complete harmony between these two powers, as represented by the speculative and political classes, and to the agreement of each of these classes amongst themselves.[78] The circumstance that Europe was, at the time when he wrote, in a state of unparalleled anarchy, he attributed, without hesitation, to the confusion at present existing in both these departments.[79] In the first, a conflict is fiercely raging between the supporters of the old theology and the scientific professors of the new philosophy;[80] in the second, the feudal classes are vainly seeking to retain a power which the growing influence of industrialism is wrenching from their grasp.[81] Nor can the spiritual power in its present divided condition possess the influence it should rightfully exert over the temporal power through the legitimate channel of public opinion.

[76] See Appendix, No. 27.   [77] Ib. No. 28.   [78] Ib. No. 29.
[79] Ib. No. 30.   [80] Ib. No. 31.   [81] Ib. No. 32.

When both are in this manner divided within themselves and against each other, the state of Europe can
afford us no astonishment. Every effect is produced
by an adequate cause, and here, at least, we have found
one of magnitude. To re-establish harmony amongst
the spiritual or speculative classes was the great object
which Saint-Simon proposed to himself, because, then
alone can the influence be regained which is necessary
for the restoration of order to Europe.[82]

V.

He suggested, therefore, that a new spiritual power
be established, copied from the palmiest days of Catholicism, but substituting physicism, or positive philosophy, for Christian theology.[83] The clergy of this new
religion were to be scientific scholars;[84] they were to
be governed from a central authority,[85] before which
the nations of the earth were to bow their heads, and
by which all their rivalries were to be appeased.[86] To
every temple there was to be a college attached, where
the future generations would be taught the new theology;[87] and the new theology will be none other than
the most recent results of science, for in the volume of
that book alone can we hope to unravel the gigantic
mysteries by which we are surrounded, and of which
we are ourselves a part.[88]

---

[82] See Appendix, No. 33. [83] *Ib*. No. 34. [84] *Ib*. No. 35.
[85] *Ib*. No. 36. [86] *Ib*. No. 37. [87] *Ib*. No. 38. [88] *Ib*. No. 39.

VI.

Nor were the maxims of a positive morality to be forgotten.[89] The test of excellence was no longer to be the exercise of certain sickly virtues,[90] but the discharge of practical duties, from whence substantial benefit may accrue to mankind.[91] Above all, the religious obligation of labour was to be enforced, and the anathema of public opinion was to descend with merited severity upon the idle rich.[92] Society was thus to be divided into three classes,—the temporal power in the hands of the industrial classes, the spiritual power in the hands of the learned, whose united duty it would be to prevent the people from falling into disorder; while, over both people and temporal rulers, the spiritual power—or physicist clergy—would exercise the supreme control derived from public opinion, and, being formed upon positive or scientific knowledge, it would be unanimous and inquisitorial. Such were the doctrines taught by Saint-Simon from 1803 to 1818, at which latter date he was joined by Auguste Comte, then twenty years of age. The reader who is familiar with the speculations of Comte, both in his early Positive phase, and in his later theological phase, will at once perceive how analogous are many of his views with those expounded above.

It will be recollected that M. Comte has ascribed

[89] See Appendix, No. 40.   [90] *Ib.* No. 41.   [91] *Ib.* No. 42.
[92] *Ib.* No. 43.

an essay to 1819, which, however, he first published 1824.
at a much later date. In it he has observed that the
same law applies to politics as to the other sciences;
and that it would be absurd for those who are ignorant of astronomy to exercise any "liberty of private
judgment" respecting the recurrence of a comet, and
if the same is not the case in politics it is only because
the professors of that science are divided among themselves, and therefore inspire no confidence. The same
idea was implied by Saint-Simon when he showed that
the disorganization of society is to be attributed to
the conflict which exists among the "spiritual classes,"
and when he pressed the necessity of raising politics
to the rank of a positive science, in order to terminate
the present disorder. But the aptness of the illustra-
tion, if indeed it were first used by M. Comte, was
fully appreciated by Saint-Simon, and we find it occur
with due prominence in the ' Organisateur' of 1820.

The ' Système Industriel' has a very exceptional interest, for it enables us to witness the birth of what became subsequently the doctrine of M. Comte respecting the influence of metaphysics upon the evolution
of ideas.[93] We are told by Saint-Simon that the transition in the "temporal power" from feudalism to industrialism, and in the "spiritual power" from theology to Positivism, could not have been effected without the assistance of an intermediate state wherein the

[93] See Appendix, No. 44.

ideas peculiar to both would appear for a time to be reconciled. Accordingly, as regards the first, there arose a class of persons called "légistes," whose business it was to conciliate the pretensions of the feudal classes with the rising influence of the Commons.[94] The result was Parliamentary or Representative Government, and the simultaneous growth of a number of curious maxims—such, for instance, as that of "the Sovereignty of the People," and their right to "liberty."[95] As regards the second, a body of metaphysicians appeared, whose duty it became to effect a compromise between the old theology and the new philosophy;[96] and their labours finally led in one part of Europe to Protestantism, and in France to the rise of a critical school of philosophers.[97] The maxims they introduced were also of a purely metaphysical character, such, for instance, as "liberty of private judgment."[98] Saint-Simon even went so far as to suggest that each particular science had passed through a metaphysical state, analogous to that which has characterized the evolution of human thought in the great departments of philosophy and politics.[99] The peculiar mission of the present century he declares to be the reconstruction of both upon a Positive basis.[100]

Now, if these recent speculations of Saint-Simon were disconnected from those that had preceded them,

---

[94] See Appendix, No. 45. [95] *Ib.* No. 46. [96] *Ib.* No. 47.
[97] *Ib.* No. 48. [98] *Ib.* No. 49. [99] *Ib.* No. 50. [100] *Ib.* No. 51.

it might be said that they are due to the influence of Comte; but the fact, on the contrary, is that all his writings have tended in this direction. He had already attacked lawyers with great energy; he had pointed out clearly enough the function they had to perform, and he had intimated that their mission was now terminated. A great part of his life had been devoted to ingenious speculations as to how the people might be restrained in their liberty and deprived of their sovereignty, and he had already acknowledged that parliamentary government could only be a transitory form. He had frequently pointed to Protestantism as the direct consequence of scientific inquiry, and his views on Positivism are too well known to leave any room for supposing that he ever considered Protestantism as more than transitory; we have also seen that ever since 1808 his efforts had been consistently directed towards the one object of rendering all the particular sciences positive, with a view to the elaboration of a positive philosophy and politics. The fact, however, remains that these views were published to the world by Saint-Simon in 1820, and nothing to the same effect was written by Comte till 1822.

M. Littré has already noticed some of the opinions common to both writers. Among other incidental similarities there occur the following:

1. They both insisted upon the great importance of the power of scientific prediction.

2. They both conjectured that if man were to disappear from the earth, the animal next in rank might rise to perfection.

3. They both agreed as to the intellectual revolution effected by Descartes' erroneous theory of Vortices.

4. They both perceived the subordination of the study of organic to that of inorganic bodies.

5. They both attribute to Protestantism a reaction in favour of Deism, and ascribe the growth of Positivism in France to the circumstance that she escaped the Reformation.

6. They both rejected the applicability of the word "materialism" to their respective philosophies.

Enough has perhaps been said to satisfy an unprejudiced reader that M. Comte was more indebted to Saint-Simon than has been generally supposed, or than his disciples will be ready to admit.[101]

Many years previous to the period at which we have now arrived, Saint-Simon undertook the laborious task of completing the positivity of knowledge by banishing supernaturalism from physiology. He conceived also the necessity of forming a positive philosophy to replace the current theologies, and to restore order and authority to society. He justly estimated his own powers as too feeble for the accomplishment of any such design, and he looked forward

[101] See Appendix, No. 52.

with hope to a successor who would be more competent.[102] It is only natural to suppose that he imparted his enthusiasm to his pupil, and M. Comte was thus enabled to conceive and to undertake in his youth the immense labour to which he devoted his life. The fame of the master has been completely eclipsed by that of the pupil.

"On a souvent remarqué," said Saint-Simon, as if by anticipation of his own fate, "que l'exécution d'une grande entreprise, de quelque nature que ce soit, est presque toujours attribuée en totalité à celui qui y a mis la dernière main, quoiqu'il n'y ait contribué d'ordinaire que pour la plus petite partie."[103]

It is true that the "dernière main" has not yet been put to the Positive Philosophy, but the share Saint-Simon contributed to the edifice should not be forgotten.

It is of course impossible to maintain that the whole of the Positive Philosophy may be found in the writings of Saint-Simon. Comte added much that is purely his own and much that he borrowed from other sources; but he was very far from the truth when he said that his relation with Saint-Simon "n'avait comporté d'autre résultat que d'entraver mes méditations spontanées, antérieurement guidées par Condorcet, sans me procurer d'ailleurs aucune acquisition."

Besides the similarity in many points of doctrine,

---

[102] See Appendix, No 53. [103] 'Œuvres,' vol. xxi. p. 87.

1824. there was also much similarity of character between the two men. They were both excessively vain; they were both satisfied to live upon the generosity of their friends; they both separated from their wives; they both attempted to commit suicide; they both drew up elaborate systems for the reorganization of society; they were both firmly convinced that a few years would witness the triumph of their respective schemes; they were both the founders of a new religion; they both wrote hastily and corrected little, and they were both therefore led into much error. But Comte matured his opinions by long thought and profound study, and afterwards pursued his task steadily till he brought it to a successful termination; while Saint-Simon, on the contrary, was never tired of beginning a new work which he had neither the patience nor the ability to complete. Comte was correct in his estimate when he classed his former master "parmi les hommes d'imagination, non parmi les philosophes, concevant vite, n'achevant rien, et changeant facilement de vues et de direction."

We have now reached the close of Saint-Simon's career. In the early part of 1825, he published a collection of 'Opinions Littéraires,' with the assistance of M. Olinde Rodrigue, who then occupied the position left vacant by Comte. This work was followed by a first instalment of the 'Nouveau Christianisme,' in which the dying philosopher sought to develope the

"partie sentimentale et religieuse" of his doctrine. 1824.
He did not live to complete the task; but the frag-
ment became, after his death, the gospel of a new religious sect, who called themselves by his name. The
creed, as left by its founder, resolved itself mainly
into a belief in the progress of mankind, and the
morality that was inculcated had reference to the obligation that resulted to labour in that direction.

Saint-Simon died in May, at the age of sixty-five,
and the men who assembled round his grave, at Père-
la-Chaise, formed a nucleus from whence his religious
and political doctrines have since been disseminated
throughout every European country, and along the
distant valley of the Nile.

PART II.

SAINT-SIMONISM.

SAINT-SIMONISM.

—◆—

"Nous ne sommes pas de Chrétiens, notre royaume est de ce monde."—
Œuvres, iv. 41.

I.

IN the first part I have explained at length the view   1825. taken by Saint-Simon of human history. I have shown how he maintained that at the origin of our race man was only removed from the lower animals by a slight and purely physical superiority. From that moment to the present hour he has continued to progress, and the course he has followed has been guided by a natural law of evolution. Such is the doctrine upon which the Saint-Simonian religion is founded. And if, indeed, the theory of progress be true, it will necessarily exercise a powerful influence upon existing theological conceptions, and may even modify our ideal of a religious life. For it is sufficiently evident that many of our opinions upon these points take their origin from the totally opposite doctrines of the Garden

1825. of Eden and the Fall of Man. These fables fill the first act of the great theological drama of human affairs, and if they are omitted much that remains will lose its significance. But Paradise, according to Saint-Simon, is nowhere to be found in the past, although it may yet be realized in the far distant future; and the original condition of man, so far from being one of innocence and perfection, was characterized by absolute degradation and barbarity. His conduct since that period has been precisely the reverse of what was supposed; for he has fallen from no high estate into sin and misery, but he is slowly rising out of that condition to one of purity and happiness. Nor is there any reason to suppose that he has violated the law of God, and that his disobedience has shaded any part of the loveliness of nature. On the contrary, he has followed his appointed course according to the law of his being, against which, indeed, no resistance could permanently avail. The foundation is thus destroyed, upon which rest the current opinions respecting the relation between man and God; for if we have been guilty of no disobedience why should we have incurred His displeasure? and if we have fulfilled our place in nature, for what reason are we the objects of His wrath? If we adopt this changed view of human affairs we are delivered from the gloomy terror that must affect our lives, so long as we believe that the frown of heaven is above

us, and the fires of hell before us. We are restored to 1825.
a sense of our own dignity, and rescued from that abject humility which impedes the free play of the faculties upon whose exercise our worldly prosperity mainly
depends. Upon the same supposition the legitimate
sphere of religious duty may be somewhat altered.
Under the old theological system our efforts were very
properly directed to regain the favour we were said to
have lost; and inasmuch as the Fall produced a total
change in our nature, it was inferred that if we acted
directly contrary to our present inclinations, we should
probably approach once more to our primitive condition. Under the new theological system, however,
our activities will be employed to execute the Will of
Heaven, as it is manifested in the known Order of
Nature. The upward progress of our race is a part of
that order, and it becomes our duty, therefore, to lend
to it our human aid. Thus the ideal of a religious life
will no longer consist in the acquisition of a type of
character, whose excellence is perhaps questionable,
and at best is purely imaginative; but it will consist
in the active discharge of the duties of life, so as to
add something, however small, to the knowledge or
to the wealth, upon which the progress of civilization depends. In other words, a religious life will
be devoted to improve the condition of man upon
earth, and thereby to fulfil the beneficent design of
his Maker, and not to the practice of austerities, or

1825. any similar device by which superstitious men have sought to avert the anger of God. As the Fall of Man is the central conception of one system, his Progress is the central conception of the other. The object of religious effort is transferred from heaven to earth; it is not directed to regain a Paradise Lost, but to advance our earthly lives nearer to the perfection to which they slowly move from age to age.[1] "Le véritable Christianisme," said Saint-Simon, "doit rendre les hommes heureux, non-seulement dans le ciel, mais sur la terre." Accordingly in the Saint-Simonian religion the most important principle of morality was the obligation of labour. It will seem strange to those who are accustomed to consider devotional exercises, and the acquisition of an unworldly character, as the noblest conception of religion, to be told that in these alone there can be no salvation. For the pursuit of knowledge and the faithful exercise of an earthly calling constitute the true service of God, and those who neglect to fulfil these obligations are in the position of the unprofitable servant against whom the anger of the Lord was kindled, because he had buried his talent in the ground.

We have already seen how Saint-Simon intended to apply these principles to the reorganization of the

---

[1] "L'humanité porte en elle sa brutalité originelle, mais elle s'en purifie et s'en délivre progressivement; de génération en génération elle étend le domaine du bien et rétrécit celui du mal."—*La Vie Éternelle*, par Enfantin, éd. Bib. Utile, p. 53.

clergy. He pointed out that as the truly religious object of life is first to acquire knowledge and then to apply it usefully, it becomes evident that the most eminent persons who are so employed are in truth our natural leaders and teachers. Indeed the revolution which he desired to effect has already taken place in reality, though not in name. Those who guide the thought of intelligent laymen in the present day are no longer the clergy; they have been left far behind in every department of human knowledge, and they impede rather than stimulate the intellectual development of the age. It is the great lay scholars who are the real instructors of men, and whose noble works in literature and science have replaced both pulpit and confessional. When therefore Saint-Simon declared that scholars, artists and men of business, are the true priests of the future, and positive knowledge the foundation for theology, he but anticipated a conclusion to which opinion is already gravitating.[2] Both his theology and his principle of morality are likewise gaining ground. All the recent discoveries in many depart-

---

[2] "Nous avons fait entrevoir un temps qui ne pouvait être éloigné, où les sciences, dégagées de l'influence des dogmes de la critique et envisagées d'une manière plus large, plus générale qu'elles ne le sont aujourd'hui, bien loin de continuer à être regardées comme destinées à combattre la religion, ne se présenteraient plus que comme le moyen donné à l'esprit humain de connaître les lois par lesquelles Dieu gouverne le monde, de connaître, en d'autres termes, le plan de la providence."—*Doctrine de Saint-Simon, Exposition,* 1ᵉ *année* 1829, 2nd ed. (Paris, 1830), p. 417.

1825.   ments of science have confirmed the great doctrine of
progress, and the speculations of Mr. Darwin have
lately given to the theory a very remarkable extension.
The moral obligation of labour, as a religious duty, is
not yet so distinctly recognized, and there are many
who still consider an unchaste act as a more grievous
sin than an idle life, and who fancy that they have
fulfilled all the law and the prophets, when they can
persuade themselves that they believe a series of in-
tricate propositions, and when they have acquired
a type of character neither useful nor agreeable for
terrestrial purposes.   But even this ideal of a religious
life is gradually disappearing under the influence of the
great sceptical movement which is so beneficially modi-
fying ancient superstitions, and we may look forward
with confidence to the natural evolution of a moral code,
and of a religious spirit that will transcend those that
have gone before, even as our knowledge exceeds that
out of which all previous systems have been formed.[3]

Saint-Simon wrote the 'Nouveau Christianisme,'
with a view to convert the Christian clergy to these
opinions, and also to supply a gospel for the new faith ;
he, however, died before its completion, and the frag-

_____

[3] " Nous venons proclamer que l'humanité a un avenir religieux ;
que la religion de l'avenir sera plus grande, plus puissante que toutes
celles du passé ; qu'elle sera, comme celles qui l'ont précédée, la synthèse
de toutes les conceptions de l'humanité . . . que non-seulement elle
dominera l'ordre politique, mais que l'ordre politique sera, dans son
ensemble, une institution religieuse."—*Doctrine*, p. 334.

ment he has left is mainly critical. Religion is, he says, 1825.
progressive; the injunction to "Love one another,"
resumes all that is truly divine in Christianity. For centuries the inculcation of this command produced upon
society the most beneficial results; it destroyed slavery,
it softened manners, it even elevated the poor and base-
born to the Papal crown, to be the equal or the superior
of the richest and noblest. But the principle is now
sufficiently established in theory, and it should descend
from the region of eloquent declamation, to be worked
out in every department of human affairs. In other
words, Christianity having prepared the way, by gaining acceptance for the principle, it is reserved for the
New Christianity to carry that principle into effect by
such practical measures as will really "ameliorate the
moral and physical condition of the greatest number."
Here however the Christian clergy refuse to lend their
assistance. Now they lag behind the age: they ex-
pend their energies upon frivolous disputes; they contribute in no degree to the improvement of society,
they even seek to arrest its progress; so far from
rising against the evils of life, and leading the people
to their conquest, they fold their arms in idleness, and
utter pernicious maxims of submission and resignation
to what they falsely call the will of God. They even
dare to denounce the knowledge that can alone save
humanity from manifold forms of suffering, and they
seek to perpetuate ignorance and credulity in order

that their cherished fancies may not be disturbed. It is not therefore to them that mankind will henceforth entrust their welfare; but to those whose knowledge and whose pursuits can guide towards the great religious object of human improvement upon earth.

The application of these principles to social institutions was not a little remarkable. In order to remove both ignorance and poverty, it was proposed that the State should become the Universal Legatee, and indeed the Common Parent of all. Former revolutions, it was said, have swept away every privilege of birth with the exception of the right of inheritance, and to it are to be ascribed the unjust inequalities that still continue in society. "Libre!" they exclaimed with irony, " quand on manque de pain! Égaux en droits! lorsque l'un a le droit de vivre sans travailler, et que l'autre, s'il ne travaille pas, n'a plus que le droit de mourir!"[4] A few enjoy the privileges of education and the power of capital, and they thus start at the outset of life with great advantages; but the vast majority are heavily weighted by ignorance and poverty. Hence society has introduced an artificial inequality, which justice imperatively demands shall be removed.[5] For this

---

[4] " L'ouvrier," they said, " se présente comme le descendant direct de l'esclave et du serf: sa personne est libre, il n'est plus attaché à la glèbe, mais c'est là tout ce qu'il a conquis, et, dans cet état d'affranchissement légal, il ne peut subsister qu'aux conditions qui lui sont imposées par une classe peu nombreuse."—*Doctrine*, p. 176.

[5] " Les hommes se trouvent aujourd'hui destinés à l'élévation morale

reason private inheritance will be abolished in favour
of the State, which will undertake in return to perform
all the duties of parents, but with a skill and an im-
partiality peculiarly its own.   A government department analogous to a foundling hospital will be established, to which there will be attached a vast organization of skilled officials, whose business it will be
to ascertain the capacity of each child, to adapt its
education thereto, and afterwards to place it in the
world in the position best suited to its ability. At that
period every one will also receive a dowry : the amount
being regulated according to the necessities of the re-
cipient in the walk of life that has been selected for
him. The race will thenceforth be to the swift and the
battle to the strong, for it is no part of the scheme
to counteract the inequalities of nature, but only to remove those that have been imposed by the injustice of

ou à la dépravation, aux lumières ou à l'ignorance, à la richesse ou à la
misère, *d'après le hasard seul de la naissance*, c'est-à-dire d'après la
condition dans laquelle se trouvaient fortuitement eux-mêmes les parents
dont ils sont nés. Aucune classe ne sera plus vouée à la dépravation, à
l'ignorance, à la misère ; il n'y aura plus entre les hommes que des
inégalités d'amour, de science et de richesse; et ces inégalités ne seront
plus déterminées par le hasard de la naissance. Toutes les chances
d'avancement seront égales pour tous au moment où ils arriveront à la
vie ; car à ce moment la même éducation sera mise à la portée de tous
et le fonds de la richesse sociale leur sera également ouvert ; les inégalités qui s'établiront entre eux ne seront donc que l'expression fidèle
de celles même de leurs vocations primitives. Chacun alors sera véritablement *placé* dans le monde *selon sa capacité et recompensé selon
ses œuvres.*"—*Œuvres de Saint-Simon et d'Enfantin*, 23 vols., (Paris,
1865–9) vol. i. p. 229.

society. It will of course be objected that such a system would destroy the motive for industry, because the majority of men are actuated by purely personal ambition. But the Saint-Simonians contended that such would not be the case; for industry will become an enthusiasm as war and religion once were, and men will then be just as ready to sacrifice their lives in its service. It was thought that these changes in the organization of society would produce a vast diminution of crime, so that justice would be adequately administered by the chiefs of the three leading departments of knowledge, art, and industry. The government itself would be constituted in the same manner, for it was to be composed of the great scholars, artists and men of business who had attained to that eminent position in virtue of their transcendent capacity, and to whom therefore the prosperity of the nation could be safely entrusted. "Pour nous," they said, "il n'y a pas de chef par droit de conquête, ni même par droit de naissance, mais seulement par droit de capacité morale, intellectuelle et industrielle. Dans la société telle que nous la concevons, tout homme qui juge ses inférieurs a aussi des supérieurs qui le jugent." "Le chef politique est législateur et juge, il conçoit le réglement d'ordre, et en détermine l'application; il est la loi vivante, il est l'organe de la louange et de la réprobation sociales."[6] The changes such a system of society

---

[6] 'Doctrine de Saint-Simon,' p. 46.

would effect are of course very great, and the disciples
of Saint-Simon, many of whom were gifted with
much eloquence and enthusiasm, painted in glowing
language the happiness that will shortly become
universal, when wars shall be unknown, when ignorance shall be dispelled, and when poverty and the inequalities of birth shall have been removed; and they
contrasted it with the fearful struggle for life in which
we are at present involved. Looking back upon the
long course of history they were able to investigate
the general tendencies it exhibited,[7] and from the study
they derived a sure hope that in time their dreams
may indeed be realized; for they saw that society
is moving onwards with certain steps towards peaceful associations. As individuals have been united into
families, and families into tribes, and tribes into
nations, so will nations be finally united into one
common humanity; and as the object of their union
was formerly for robbery and murder, so will it be
eventually for purposes of industry. They inferred
also that the existing system of private enterprise and
unlimited competition corresponds in industry to the
period of Feudalism when the right of private war
existed, and as the latter was finally abolished and
gave place to a central military government, so will our

[7] "Vous êtes convaincus que toute prévision qui ne serait pas appuyée sur une tendance de l'humanité, rigoureusement constatée, devrait
être repoussée comme le fruit d'une imagination malade, faible et
rêveuse."—*Doctrine*, p. 350.

existing industrial organization be gradually brought under the control of the State.[8]

There was one part of the Saint-Simonian doctrine that exposed the disciples to the charge of immorality. As they entirely rejected the doctrine of the Fall, with its long train of singular consequences, they saw no reason to believe that the temperate indulgence of the passions was in any way iniquitous, and they were not very respectful to the institution of marriage. They seemed to fancy that its object was to make life more agreeable; and they knew that the contrary was not unfrequently its result. They, therefore, inferred that when the object had failed the contract might lawfully terminate, and the parties be permitted to return to the desolation of single life, or even to make a fresh experiment in matrimony. Of course, so long as marriage is considered to be a religious institution of a very solemn character, there is no hope that it will be regulated with a view to anything so insignificant as human happiness; but it is not strange that the

[8] "De nos jours ce principe de liberté, de concurrence, de guerre, existe entre les commerçans et fabricans d'un même pays, il existe de province à province, de ville à ville, de fabrique à fabrique, disons plus encore de boutique à boutique. La féodalité mit un terme à l'anarchie militaire en liant les ducs, comtes, barons et tous les propriétaires indépendants, hommes d'armes, par des services et une protection réciproques . . . de même les éléments du travail pacifique tendent aujourd'hui à se constituer en une seule société ayant ses chefs, sa hiérarchie, une organisation et une destinée communes."—*Doctrine*, p. 197. Compare 'Colonisation d'Algérie,' par Enfantin, (Paris, 1843,) p. 273.

Saint-Simonians, who only regarded its social aspect, 1825. should be influenced by that consideration.

It cannot be said that they had any intention of reducing woman to be the plaything of man, for their efforts were systematically directed to place her in a position of perfect equality with him, in regard to religious, social, and political rights. In fact, so far did they carry their views in this direction that they believed that no religious or profane undertaking could be permanently successful without her co-operation; and they even entered into speculations concerning the androgynous character of the person of God, which were highly remarkable on the part of educated men, in the present century.

In one respect, indeed, they exhibited very unusual good sense. In their publications and discourses they did not advocate those sudden and sweeping changes, so pleasing to radical reformers; they sought on the contrary to modify existing institutions, so as to lead by insensible degrees towards the result they contemplated. Their views on marriage, for example, they endeavoured to graft upon the present institution by increasing the facilities for divorce. The first step towards the endowment of the State was to be the abolition of collateral inheritance in its favour, and the augmentation of the tax upon direct succession. The benefit of capital was to be largely extended by the multiplication of banks; and a liberal measure of

1825.   national education would remove many of the disabilities now arising from ignorance. In a similar spirit
they advocated free trade, as the surest means of link-
ing the various nations together in the bonds of perpetual peace.[9]

Such were the leading principles of Saint-Simonism,
and those who are acquainted with the tendency of
modern thought will be at no loss to account for the
influence they exercised upon men who to youth and
inexperience united a generous desire to improve the
condition of society, and a profound distrust in the
power of existing institutions to accomplish the task.
Lacordaire even thought that in a religious point of
view it was the most important movement since the
time of Luther.[10]

II.

Olinde Rodrigue was accustomed to say, though
with some exaggeration, that he was the only disciple
Saint-Simon had left. It is true, indeed, that the
earliest steps towards the formation of the sect of
Saint-Simonians are mainly to be ascribed to his exer-

---

[9] 'Doctrine de Saint-Simon,' pp. 50, 205 ; 'Œuvres,' vol. iv. p. 18.
On the influence of the Saint-Simonians upon political economy in
France, see the opinions of M. Blanqui, Hist. de l'Écon. Pol. vol. ii.
ch. 43, and of M. Granier de Cassagnac, quoted in ' Œuvres de Saint-
Simon et d'Enfantin,' vol. xiii. p. 32.

[10] ' Œuvres de Saint-Simon et d'Enfantin,' vol. xiii. p. 251.

tions; there remained, however, a few friends who were ready to second his initiative. Indeed, their zeal was so great that Dr. Bailly, in his funeral oration, thought it necessary to guard against their extravagance. " Si chacun de vous," he said, " se joignait à moi dans ce moment pour restituer à notre maître commun ce que vous tenez de lui, si chacun de vous, entraîné par le sentiment de conviction qui me domine, le proclamait dans chacune des directions que vous suivez, comme l'auteur des idées les plus belles et les plus fécondes qui aient jamais été créées, vous feriez un acte de justice sans doute ; mais vous ne parviendriez jamais à faire adopter une opinion qui paraîtrait dictée par l'enthousiasme et l'exagération." [11] Shortly before his death, Saint-Simon had endeavoured to establish a newspaper, with a view to disseminate his opinions ; he had intended to have called it the ' Producteur,' but the scheme had failed from want of money. Rodrigue now suggested to those who were mourning with him that the best tribute they could pay to their lost friend would be to undertake such a publication. The idea was readily acceded to, and shares of 1000 francs each were sold. Lafitte bought 10 ; Rodrigue and others 3 each ; the total number of subscribers exceeded 20. Of these there were many who, besides money, contributed also articles ; and they exercised an important influence on

[11] *Ib.* vol. i. p. 125.

the future development of the new sect. The most remarkable were MM. Enfantin and Bazard, who shortly became the high-priests of the new faith, and who therefore require special notice.

Barthélemy-Prosper Enfantin was born at Paris in 1796. His father had been a banker, but having failed in business he retired, and accepted a small office at the University. In 1813, Barthélemy entered the Polytechnic School, where he at once gained the affection of all his associates; he also formed the acquaintance of Olinde Rodrigue, who was his *répétiteur* in mathematics, in which study Enfantin was more proficient than in classics. During the "Hundred Days" he served as secretary to his relation, General Saint-Cyr-Nugues. At the termination of the war he went into business with another of his relations, who was a wine merchant; and he occasionally travelled in Germany for the firm. He afterwards went to St. Petersburg as clerk in a bank. While there he renewed the acquaintance of some of his former comrades at the Polytechnic School, and they spent the long winter evenings together for purposes of study; they read the works of such authors as Cabanis, Condorcet, Volney, and Bentham. Enfantin became engrossed in questions of political economy and finance, and he addressed an essay upon the subject to the Academy of Sciences at Lyons; he also drew up a scheme for the liquidation of the public debt, which he communi-

cated to M. de Villèle and to M. Lafitte. He was
obliged, for family reasons, to return to France in 1822,
and he was then accorded audiences by both these
gentlemen, but with what result does not appear. He
finally got the appointment of cashier to the Caisse
Hypothécaire, which he held till his apostolic labours
occupied the whole of his attention. In 1823, he
became acquainted with the writings of Saint-Simon,
and subscribed to the Catéchisme des Industriels; but
he only met the author upon one occasion, when he
was introduced by Olinde Rodrigue. The character
of Enfantin is an interesting problem; he was an
enthusiast, concerning whose sincerity there can be
little dispute. He displayed much of the strength,
and, it must be confessed, much of the weakness inse-
parable from such a disposition : he firmly believed
that he was a prophet; not only the bearer of a celes-
tial message, but the very incarnate living Word of
God. He was at once sceptical and credulous : he
rejected Christian theology, yet he believed in the
noble mission of his inspired predecessors. At one
time he indulged in the strangest speculations concerning the sex of God; at another he attained to the
highest conceptions of Pantheism. The influence this
strange man acquired is in the highest degree remarkable when we consider over whom it was exercised.
Sceptical men of business, distinguished officers, ardent young lawyers, learned professors, and disciples

of Voltaire were among his followers. He ruled despotically over their lives and thoughts; he induced them to renounce their wives or their mistresses, and to lead an ascetic life; he withdrew them from refined society, and forced them to share in the coarsest toil; he compelled them to undergo the humiliation of public confessions, and he received from them the honours and the reverence accorded to a Divine teacher. Yet his intellectual powers were inferior to those possessed by some of his disciples. His eloquence derives its sublimity in a great degree from its obscurity, and the apparent subtility of his writings is due chiefly to a profusion of capital letters and italics. His early life was clouded by many misfortunes, and they had deeply influenced his opinions. When his father became a bankrupt, the family was exposed to much distress. His brother, a young artist of promise, to whom he was ardently attached, fell a victim to the treachery of the Italian climate. But worse than all, the woman whom he had hoped to marry was refused to him, because of the disgrace that followed his father's bankruptcy; he never really recovered from this misfortune. The fugitive attachments he afterwards formed could not heal the cruel wound, and his subsequent dreams concerning the *femme messie* may perhaps be ascribed to the longings of an unsatisfied heart. His views were noble and generous, and he advocated them with all the sincerity of genuine en-

thusiasm and the boldness of matchless self-confidence.
It was natural that they should fascinate young men of
an ardent temperament, who burned with a chivalrous
desire to redress the evils of the world. They were
readily charmed by a prophet whose countenance was
remarkable for its dignity and repose, and whose affectionate disposition inspired them with boundless confidence and fervour. It must be admitted also that
both his religious and political opinions contained a
large amount of truth ; but his vanity has invested
them with an appearance of absurdity, for he delighted
in fantastic dresses, in solemn processions and imposing ceremonies ; and he exposed himself to the
ridicule of the world by permitting his disciples to
speak to him of the majesty of his countenance and
the divine brightness of his smile.

M. Bazard, who for a time shared an equal authority with Enfantin, was of a totally opposite character.
When he joined Saint-Simonism he was thirty-six years
of age and ever since he was sixteen he had depended
exclusively upon his own exertions. His life had been
that of an active politician. When the approach of the
Allies threatened the safety of Paris, he was conspicuous
among its defenders. At a later period he became one
of the seven founders of Carbonarism in France.[12]

---

[12] Compare " La Charbonnerie," par Trélat, in ' Paris Révolution-
naire,' 1838. Louis Blanc, ' Histoire de Dix Ans,' vol. i. p. 92.
' Œuvres de Saint-Simon et d'Enfantin,' vol. vii. p. 53.

1825. When Dugied brought the laws of the society from
Naples, it was to Bazard, Buchez, and Flotard that the
task of adapting them to French sympathies was intrusted. It was Bazard who enlisted Lafayette in
favour of the conspiracy. He was foremost in the
most daring enterprises, and he barely escaped with
his life from Béfort. In common with many others
at that time, he thought that secret violence was the
only means of relieving the country from the reac-
tionary measures of the Bourbons. But failure led to
suspicion, and Bazard became an object of distrust to
his associates; their ingratitude drove him to misan-
thropy. "All the evil that has ever been charged
against mankind," he says, "I myself have witnessed
and cruelly suffered from." The complete failure at
Béfort, and the final disaster at Rochelle, convinced
him that no hope could be found in conspiracy; and
it was during the discouragement that followed that
he happened to meet with the works of Saint-Simon.
It was then that he resolved to devote his energies to
the peaceful reorganization of society, instead of to its
violent subversion. The mind of Enfantin was essen-
tially speculative, while that of Bazard was practical;
the business of the one was to originate theories, that
of the other to adapt them to practice; the first communicated the impulse, the other moderated it by prudence. The union of such dissimilar characters was
eminently favourable to the infant doctrine; though

as might be anticipated, it ultimately produced division. Such were two of the principal recruits obtained by the energy of Rodrigue for the staff of the 'Producteur.' It first appeared in October, 1825, as a weekly journal. The contributors met every Friday evening at the house of the editor, M. Cerclet, and it was found that their members steadily increased. They were joined at this early period by M. Transon, by M. Laurent, an accomplished author and professor, and by M. Michel Chevalier, a young engineer, who is now well known in this country as the Cobden of France. M. Comte also contributed two very able essays, " Considérations Philosophiques sur les Sciences et les Savants," and " Considérations sur le Nouveau Pouvoir Spirituel," in which he explained the leading features of his philosophy.[13] Although the paper was

---

[13] It must not be supposed, however, that he had the least sympathy for the new sect. He wrote in the 'Producteur' purely to get money; and only after he was fully assured that he would not be compromised by doing so. During the editorship of M. Cerclet any opinion might be expressed; when he was succeeded by Enfantin, Comte ceased to contribute, because the journal then became exclusively Saint-Simonian and religious. (Littré, p. 163.) Its religious aspect was at that time particularly obnoxious to Comte, and when we remember that he ended his own life as the Supreme Pontiff of Positivism, the following passage, written in 1829, is curious :—" La retour à la théologie de la part des gens qui en étaient d'abord tout-à-fait sortis, est pour moi aujourd'hui un signe irrécusable de médiocrité intellectuelle, et peut-être même de manque de véritable énergie morale." (*Ib.* p. 174.) In 1832, he added, " Je n'ai jamais hésité à aucune époque à regarder et à proclamer hautement l'influence des idées religieuses, même supposées strictement et constamment réduites à leur moindre développement, comme étant aujourd'hui chez les peuples les plus avancés le prin-

1825. thus supported by much ability, it never became
popular, and after six months' trial, M. Cerclet retired
from the editorship, and the chief direction devolved
upon M. Enfantin. It lingered till the following December. as a monthly journal, and then it expired,
having severely taxed the resources of its staff, both
in money and in health. Yet M. Rodrigue had good
cause to be satisfied with what he had already accomplished. He had rallied round him a few clever and
energetic men who had embraced the doctrines of

cipal obstacle aux grands projets de l'intelligence humaine et aux per-
fectionnements généraux de l'organisation sociale." (*Ib.* p. 194.) Upon
which M. Littré thus comments:—"Cette lettre manifesté clairement
l'aversion qu'avait alors M. Comte pour toute construction religieuse.
. . . On n'y découvre qu'une inflexible réprobation de toute religion,
sous quelque forme qu'elle se présente. La distinction entre théologie et
religion n'était pas encore née dans son esprit." (P. 197.) Compare
with this the 'Préface de l'Appendice Général,' written in 1854, in
which M. Comte states that he intended "Surtout à manifester la
parfaite harmonie des efforts qui caractérisèrent ma jeunesse avec les
travaux qu'accomplit ma maturité. . . . Quand on n'y saisit point la
relation nécessaire entre la base philosophique et la construction religieuse, les deux parties de ma carrière semblent procéder selon des directions différentes. Il convient donc de faire spécialement sentir que la
seconde se borne à réaliser la destination préparée par la première.
Cet appendice doit spontanément inspirer une telle conviction en con-
statant que, dès mon début, je tentai de fonder le nouveau pouvoir
spirituel que j'institue aujourd'hui. L'ensemble de mes premiers essais
me conduisit à reconnaître que cette opération sociale exigeait d'abord
un travail intellectuel, sans lequel on ne pourrait solidement établir la
doctrine destinée à terminer la révolution occidentale. Voilà pourquoi
je consacrai la première moitié de ma carrière à construire, d'après les
résultats scientifiques, une philosophie vraiment positive, seule base
possible de la religion universelle." (Système de Pol. Pos. vol. iv. App.
p. 1.)

Saint-Simon with enthusiasm, and who were not to be
easily discouraged. When they were deprived of their
bond of union by the failure of the 'Producteur,' they
still continued to dine together every week at the Re-
staurant Prévot, in the Palais Royal, and afterwards to
assemble in the rooms occupied by M. Rodrigue at the
Caisse Hypothécaire, of which establishment he was
the director.[14] They also maintained an extensive correspondence throughout the provinces, where their
opinions had already penetrated. At Sorèze an ardent
disciple had been gained in Rességuier; and through
his exertions Saint-Simonism spread extensively among
the doctors and lawyers of Languedoc. In Paris,
Rodrigue and his friends found the *salons* of General
Lafayette open to them; and they there enjoyed the
privilege of meeting the most eminent men in France.
Yet their views had to encounter severe opposition
from the representatives of very different parties. The
Liberals attacked them in the 'Globe,' and the clergy in
the 'Catholique.' Lamennais, Stendhal, and D'Eckstein
were unanimously arrayed against them; while Ben-
jamin Constant denounced them as the priests of
Thebes and Memphis. Indeed, their doctrines were
not likely to meet with much favour from any side:
they preached peace in the midst of violent party

---

[14] The Caisse Hypothécaire, in the Rue Neuve-Saint-Augustin, was
for a time the nucleus of the new faith. Rodrigue and Enfantin were
employed in it; and also the father of Duveyrier.

1827. strife; they advocated the paramount claims of pro-
ductive industry to a nation whose chief delight was
the destructive art of war; they were the apostles of a
religion to sceptics who cared for none, or to Christians
who were content with their own; they inculcated a
new morality to libertines who would brook no restraint,
or to theologians who believed their own ideal was
divine; and finally, they proclaimed the principle of
authority to a people who were enamoured of licence,
and who fancied themselves already oppressed by the
abuse of power. In the midst of this opposition Enfantin had to leave Paris on account of ill-health, produced by excessive labour. "L'école est comme dis-
soute," Buchez wrote to him; "vous étiez le lien qui
unissait les parties. J'ai rencontré deux fois Rodrigue
dehors et une fois dans la cour de ma maison. Je ne
vois guère Rouen. Plus de travail commun. J'ai
demandé à Rodrigue s'il travaillait à part. Point de
réponse. Bazard et Laurent demeurent trop loin.
Vous vous manquez, mon cher Enfantin "

In the following year, however, the new sect evinced
more vitality; it gained two very important members
in MM. Barrault and Fournel. The former was an
eminent professor of literature at the College of
Sorèze, and he was well known as a writer of plays,
some of which had been performed at the Théâtre
Français. He was gifted with remarkable eloquence,
and he became the leading orator of Saint-Simonism.

M. Fournel had been a distinguished pupil at the Polytechnic School, and he subsequently acquired considerable reputation as an engineer. He was made director of the great manufacturing establishment at Creuzot, in the Département de Saône-et-Loire, a highly lucrative appointment, which he subsequently resigned, in order to devote himself exclusively to the interests of the new faith. M. Bazard began a course of explanatory lectures every Wednesday evening, and he was listened to with attention by a select audience of twenty-five or thirty persons. An attempt was made to revive the ' Producteur,' and some subscriptions were promised, but the effort was premature. The increasing number of disciples, however, rendered it necessary towards the close of the year, to organize a sacred college of apostles. This illustrious order was at first composed of six of the eldest and most eminent members of the church. These were Rodrigue, Enfantin, Bazard, Buchez, Laurent and Rouen. The younger members who formed the second order assumed the name of Le Petit Mercredi, from the day upon which they were accustomed to meet; at the same time it was found that Rodrigue's room at the Caisse Hypothécaire had become too small, and they secured the use of a larger apartment in the Rue Taranne. In the following August, M. Victor Augier invited M. Laurent to join him in the publication of a weekly journal. M. Lau-

1829. rent complied, upon the condition that six or eight columns should be devoted to the treatment of religious and political questions from a Saint-Simonian point of view. The result was the appearance of 'L'Organisateur, Journal des progrès de la Science générale.' "C'est Laurent," says Enfantin, "qui a commencé contre vents et marée, sans collaborateurs même, l'Organisateur. Fatigué des lenteurs que nous mettions à reprendre le Producteur, malgré la souscription faite en 1828, pressé de publier, d'écrire, tandis que la plupart d'entre-nous discutaient et parlaient, il commença."

After a few months, however, the 'Organisateur' became the authorized and exclusive exponent of Saint-Simonism. But while the prospects of the movement were brightening from without, unhappily there arose the fiercest divisions within the precincts of the Sacred College itself; indeed, ever since its formation, it had been agitated by the dissensions of its members. Enfantin disputed with Bazard respecting the authority of sentiment in the formation of religious belief, and with the physiologist Buchez respecting the nature of God. As regards the first, he contended that man is endowed with the double faculty of feeling and reasoning, and that both are indispensable to arrive at a right judgment, so that the ideas that are derived purely from sentiment may be perfectly true, and of equal authority to those that are

capable of rational demonstration. His discussion
with Buchez illustrated one of the applications of this
theory. It appears that M. Enfantin had arrived at
the opinion, founded no doubt upon sentiment, that
the 'material manifestation' of God was under a female
as well as a male form. This important discovery led
him to the conclusion that as God is alike man and
woman, woman must of necessity be the equal of man,
and should therefore enjoy the same privileges and
authority. Indeed, no important undertaking could
be accomplished satisfactorily, except by the social
pair, so that the female element might equally blend
with the male.[16] Thus, the emancipation of woman,
which became a prominent feature in the Saint-Simonian movement, had a somewhat singular theological
origin. In addition to all this, M. Enfantin asserted
that it was perfectly evident that human life was eternal in the past as well as in the future ; though there
was no ground to suppose that the consciousness of
any former existence would be preserved. " Soyez
certain, cher ami," he wrote, " que s'absorber dans
la pensée de la perpétuation de l'individualité après
la mort, c'est s'exposer à ne songer qu'à soi durant sa

---

[16] " Les femmes à peine sorties de la servitude sont encore partout
tenues en tutelle et frappées d'interdiction religeuse, politique, civile.
Les femmes seront definitivement affranchies, l'individu social sera
l'homme et la femme ; toute fonction religieuse, scientifique, industrielle, sera exercée par un couple."—*Doctrine de Saint-Simon*. Compare ' Œuvres,' vol. iii. p. 186.

1829.   vie. Dieu nous a donné la foi, la certitude quant au fond, mais il nous commande le doute, le mystère, l'espérance seulement quant à la forme."[16] The disputes to which these opinions gave rise, led M. Buchez and M. Rouen to retire from the College; they were followed by some of the other disciples who were members of the Petit Mercredi. The ecclesiastical spirit was very strong in M. Enfantin, and he therefore looked upon these divisions with considerable satisfaction. " Il faut faire des exemples," he wrote, " dussions-nous rester douze ou quinze seulement; ceux qui seront exclus rendront autant de services dehors que dedans. Que si quelques-uns se dégoûtent pour cela de la doctrine, ils ne valent pas un regret."[17] The growth of his religious opinions exposed him to much ridicule, and caused no small pain to his friends. His cousin, General Saint-Cyr-Nugues, under whom he had served when a youth, expressed the astonishment with which he witnessed the growth of such strange opinions. " J'étais éloigné de soupçonner," he says, " que les idées religieuses s'empareraient de ton esprit. . . . Non-seulement tu crois! mais tu veux faire croire! Tu as une mission, tu es persuadé de ton apostolat, tu veux tout réformer sur la terre! Dans ton ardeur tu prétends changer la politique, refaire la morale; tu abjures toutes tes idées, tu méprises toutes les nôtres. Tu veux substituer

[16] ' La Vie Éternelle,' p. 34.   [17] ' Œuvres,' vol. ii. p. 71.

l'autorité à l'examen !"[18] Rodrigue now determined to 1830.
resign the nominal leadership of the Saint-Simonians,
for the real power had already passed into the hands
of Enfantin and Bazard, and they continued for some
time to enjoy equal authority. At the conclusion of
the proceedings, in which this change was effected,
M. Gustave d'Eichthal, formerly a pupil of Comte,
and now an ardent disciple of Saint-Simon, made a
distressing suggestion. "Rodrigue," he said, with
enthusiasm, "the Christians gave one another the kiss
of peace, why should we not do so too ? " Where-
upon the entire assembly rose, and rushed with pre-
cipitation into the arms of the self-denying apostle.

Shortly after these changes, Rodrigue was afflicted
by the loss of his brother Eugène. Eugène had been
one of the most brilliant pupils at the University of
Paris, and though he was not more than twenty-three
years of age, he had already attained to one of the
vacant seats in the Sacred College, and was the author
of a book which was much esteemed by the Saint-
Simonians. His enthusiastic disposition was neither
tempered by judgment nor experience, and he readily
accepted the most extravagant theories of his master.
He was earnestly engaged upon the conversion of a
young lady, when all at once his heart became seriously affected. His passion created much consternation
among the elder members of the college, who fancied

[18] 'Œuvres,' vol. ii. p. 49.

I

the proceeding was scarcely discreet on the part of a father of the church. He however endeared himself to all his associates, and, as he was gifted with many talents and boundless energy, his loss was severely felt. Enfantin regarded him as his most promising disciple, but piously resigned himself to the decrees of a higher power. "Glory," he said, "to God, who has placed us in the presence of death, to reveal more clearly eternal life." The vacancies in the Sacred College by defection and death were supplied by Rességuier bishop of the church of the south, Barrault and D'Eichthal. The number of novices daily increased, and it became necessary to constitute a third order, so that their instruction might proceed without interruption to the disciples of the Petit Mercredi. For the same reason, an apartment was hired in the old Hôtel de Gèvres, which was situated between the Rue Monsigny and the Passage Choiseul. The apartment was upon the second floor, below were the offices of the Société des bonnes Études; above, those of the 'Globe' newspaper; the whole hotel was soon acquired by the Saint-Simonians, and for some years it continued to be the centre of an organization whose ramifications extended throughout a great part of Europe. Enfantin quitted his room at the Caisse Hypothécaire, and established himself in the Rue Monsigny. He was joined by Transon, Cazeaux, and shortly afterwards by Jules Lechevalier, who was a very important acquisition. The office of

the 'Organisateur,' now become an exclusively Saint- 1830.
Simonian organ, was also removed to the same
place.   The public lectures were pursued with
energy; Barrault and Transon attracted numerous
ladies by their eloquence.[19]   " Lechevalier a déjà une
dizaine de néophytes à ses trousses.   Il les endoctrine
chaudement : nous avons fait en lui une très-bonne
acquisition.   Transon va également fort bien.   Filas-
sier remue ciel et terre.   Henri, ami d'Olinde et archi-
tecte, a déjà secoué les oreilles de quelques artistes ses
confrères : il est plein de zèle, et nous donnera sous
peu d'excellents frères. . . . La séance d'hier a été
bonne.   Lechevalier a enterré tous les métaphysiciens.
Bazard, Rodigue et Margerin l'entendaient de ma
chambre." [10]   Not alone in Paris, but throughout
France the same energy and enthusiasm were displayed.
Bazard went to Brittany to preach to the people.
Enfantin made a triumphant progress through the
south.   He gives a glowing description of his visita-
tion to the " bishopric of our dear friend Rességuier."
" Glory to God," he exclaims ; " glory to Saint-Simon ;
glory to our dear brethren of the south.   I have not yet
beheld all the disciples of this diocese, but still my
heart is filled with joy; we have sown in good
ground, the harvest is abundant."[21]   Toulouse, Montpellier, Castres, Sorèze, Lyons and Metz were centres

[19] 'Œuvres,' vol. ii. p. 182.
[20] Ib. vol. ii. pp. 156, 170.   [21] Ib. vol. ii. p. 77.

of propagation.   In Algeria, M. Bigot was actively
engaged in making converts, and he gained at least
one eminent disciple in Lamoricière, who like D'Eichthal, had been a pupil of Comte.   " Les ingénieurs
des mines, des ponts-et-chaussées, les ingénieurs militaires et artilleurs, enfin tout ce qui se recrute à l'École
Polytechnique est affecté du poison Saint-Simonien,
et il circule rapidement parmi les médecins et même au
barreau."[22]   Such was the triumphant position Saint-
Simonism was already assuming, when political events
supervened which greatly augmented its success.

"The holy revolt which has just been effected,"
wrote Bazard and Enfantin in July 1830, " does not
merit the name of a revolution.   No fundamental
change has occurred in the existing social organization : a few names and titles, the national ensign and
colours, certain legislative modifications that will re-
duce the kingly power to the level of a police force,—
such are the victories achieved by these days of mourning and glory."[18]   Yet they were not slow to avail
themselves of whatever advantage might be derived
from the popular effervescence.   Bazard took advantage of his acquaintance with General Lafayette to
communicate to him his views of the crisis.   The two
conspirators met after midnight ; but the suggestions
of Bazard were not very acceptable.   He proposed
that a dictatorship should be proclaimed, and that it

[22] ' Œuvres,' vol. ii. pp. 161, 162.   [23] Ib. vol. ii. p. 211.

should continue until the people were prepared by 1830.
the apostles of Saint-Simonism to undergo the social
revolution which I have already described.[24]   At the
same time he drew up a proclamation, with the concurrence of Enfantin, and caused it to be posted upon
the walls of Paris; it was eagerly read by many who
then became acquainted, for the first time, with the
political and religious doctrines of Saint-Simonism.
It was well calculated to stimulate some of the worst
passions of an ignorant mob, and to excite them to
enter upon a war of classes. "Frenchmen," it said, "you
were stronger than your nobles, or than that crowd
of idlers who lived by the sweat of your brow; it was
because you worked;' you were more moral and more
instructed than your priests, because they were ignorant
of your callings and despised them. Show them that if
you have cast them aside, it is because you can and
will only obey those who love, assist, and enlighten
you, and not those who traffic upon your misery. Tell
them that there is no longer rank, honour, or riches
to be awarded to idleness, but only to labour. They
will then understand your revolt against them for
they will perceive that you honour and promote those
only who are devoted to your advancement. Feudalism," it concludes, "will be finally extinguished,
when all the privileges of birth are, without exception,
abolished, and when every one shall be placed accord-

[24] 'Œuvres,' vol. iii. p. 6, and note.

1830. ing to his capacity, and rewarded according to his
works.   And when this new religion shall have realized upon earth the reign of God, the reign of peace
and of liberty, which the Christians have placed in
heaven alone, then the Catholic Church will have lost
its power, it will have ceased to exist."[25]

Although the Saint-Simonians could not realize
their more ambitious projects, yet the notoriety they
achieved was considerable, and the attendance at their
lectures greatly increased.[26]   The apartments in the
Rue Monsigny were filled four times a week ; Barrault
hired a large hall in the Rue Taitbout, and his eloquent lectures were attended by more than 1000 persons, of whom 200 were ladies.[27]   Besides this, meetings were held at the Athénée, in the Place de la
Sorbonne, in the great hall at the Prado, facing
the Palais de Justice, at the Salle de la Redoute, in
the Rue de Grenelle-Saint-Honoré, and also in the

[25] 'Œuvres,' vol. ii. pp. 198–200.

[26] "Le bruit que fait la doctrine est prodigieux, on en parle partout."
—Œuvres, vol. iii. p. 21.

[27] Ib. vol. iii. pp. 21, 25, 48. Louis Blanc thus describes the scene
in the Salle Taitbout:—"Autour d'une vaste salle, sous un toit de verre,
tournaient trois étages de loges.   Devant un amphithéâtre dont une
foule empressée couvrait, dès midi, tous les dimanches, les banquettes
rouges, se plaçaient sur trois rangs des hommes sérieux et jeunes, vêtus de
bleu, et parmi lesquels figuraient quelques dames en robes blanches et
en écharpes violettes.   Bientôt paraissaient, conduisant le prédicateur,
les deux Pères suprêmes, MM. Bazard et Enfantin. A leur aspect les
disciples se levaient avec attendrissement ; il se faisait parmi les spec-
tateurs un grand silence plein de recueillement ou d'ironie, et l'orateur
commençait."—Hist. de Dix Ans, vol. iii. p. 103.

Rue Tarranne, where they had first begun. In the provinces the activity continued unabated. Jules Lechevalier was lecturing at Bordeaux, " et fait merveille;" Michel Chevalier at Limoges, Lebreton at Nantes, Maréchal, Fèvre and Briard at Metz, Péreire reported favourably of Toulouse, and the bishopric of Rességuier continued to prosper. Their opinions were vigorously debated in such papers as the ' Gazette de France,' the ' Journal des Débats,' ' Le Temps,' ' Le Correspondant,' and by M. Fazy, of Geneva, in ' La Révolution.' They had published a volume of ' Exposition,' of which 800 copies were already sold, and it was entering a second edition; but even more important than this was the impending conversion of the ' Globe,' whose offices were situated above them in the Rue Monsigny. One of the editors, M. Lherminier, had been already admitted as a novice, and it was said that the remaining two, MM. Sainte-Beuve and Pierre Leroux, were also favourably inclined towards the doctrine.[28] The hopes thus afforded were finally realized in November. The ' Globe' then became a Saint-Simonian organ, and the disciples thus found themselves in possession of a daily paper of established reputation, with 1500 permanent subscribers.[29] These

[28] Lherminier did not long remain with the Saint-Simonians. In the following year he had completely abandoned their doctrines, and was engaged at the Collége de France, in delivering a course of lectures on Comparative Legislation. (Vol. iii. p. 66, and note.)

[29] It was called the ' Globe, Journal de la Doctrine de Saint-Simon,' and had as mottoes :—

1830. successes had already excited the frivolous vanity of Enfantin, who had now resolved to render himself and his followers conspicuous by dress. "Blue," he writes, "is to be, till further orders, the colour of the Saint-Simonian costume. Bazard and I are dressed in very light blue trousers and coat, with a white waistcoat. The other members of the college wear a darker shade, and the lower the rank in the hierarchy the darker the colour, till it finally reaches royal blue. Bazard and I have already appeared twice in this manner, simply to record the pretension we advance to adopt a new costume ; cela a fait bon effet." But Enfantin manifested his weakness in many other ways, equally contemptible. He suffered himself to be addressed by his disciples in language that is scarcely compatible with the sanity of the writer. M. Reynaud writes from Corsica, "Le baiser de mon père me donnera la force et sa voix l'éloquence ; j'ai toute confiance en mon père, car je sais qu'il connaît ses enfants mieux qu'ils ne se connaissent eux-mêmes, et cependant pourquoi suis-je tremblant en allant à lui ?" Another disciple carried his reverence still further : "Salut ! père, salut ! ma vie est de t'aimer, de t'étudier et de

"RELIGION.　　SCIENCE.　　INDUSTRIE.

"ASSOCIATION UNIVERSELLE.

"Toutes les institutions sociales doivent avoir pour but l'amélioration morale, intellectuelle et physique de la classe la plus nombreuse et la plus pauvre.

"Tous les priviléges de naissance, sans exception, sont abolis.

"A chacun selon sa capacité, à chaque capacité selon ses œuvres."— *L. Reybaud,* ' *Socialistes Modernes,*' 7th ed. (Paris, 1864), vol. i. p. 108·

te servir. Salut ! tu t'avance comme un géant divin, 1830.
et tu nous entraînes sur tes pas. O mon père ! je suis
autour de toi comme le satellite auprès de sa planète ;
et quand tu verses sur le monde que Dieu t'a donné
les flots de lumière qui t'inondent, ton fils, brillant à
tes côtés, se réjouit aussi de son modeste éclat. Tu me
réjouiras d'une lumière nouvelle. Mon père ! mon père !
je le sens, le jour de ton hymen est proche, et déjà près
de toi j'ai vu le trône de ma mère."[30] The extravagant language of the disciples was fully equalled by
that of the master. He affected an ecclesiastical
dialect, absurd enough in the mouths of those who
consider themselves required by their profession to
adopt it, but supremely ridiculous on the part of who-
ever is under no such painful obligation. At the same
time he began to arrogate a supremacy that caused
his more ardent disciples infinite pleasure. On the
last day of the year he delivered an "allocution," in
which he undertook to discriminate the particular capacity of his principal followers, and to appoint them
their various tasks accordingly. "Laurent et Barrault,
vous êtes la voix de notre amour : prêchez ! Jules et
Carnot, vous êtes notre parole de science : enseignez !
Duveyrier, d'Eichthal, Michel—l'Organisateur, le Globe
sont à vous : écrivez ! Claire Bazard, vous êtes la première de nos filles, l'avenir de toutes les femmes vous
est remis : donnez nous des filles."[31] Mme. Bazard
had taken exception to one of the ladies whom a dis-

---

[30] 'Œuvres,' vol. iii. p. 80.　　　[31] Ib. vol. iii. pp. 68–71.

1880.   ciple had sought to introduce into the sacred community. This circumstance afforded Enfantin another
opportunity of displaying the authority he claimed.
It appears that Jules Lechevalier had formed a friend-
ship for a young actress whose reputation, according
to the prejudices of society, was slightly tarnished.
Mme. Bazard wrote a letter, in which she evinced
much sympathy for ladies of that particular character;
but expressed her repugnance to be brought into intimate association with them, and the danger that might
accrue to the infant church, if it came to be believed
by the world that it favoured a relaxed code of morals.
The question was warmly disputed in the Sacred
College, and Enfantin delivered himself with such
authority, that the day after his discourse, when
D'Eichthal met Laurent in the library, they rushed
with enthusiasm into one another's arms, exclaiming,
" Le pape se fait." [32]

From that period till the final schism of Bazard,
the subject continued to be fiercely disputed; but the
"pope" had embraced the cause of free-love, and his
influence secured its triumph.

The new year was begun with an attempt to carry
the gospel into foreign lands. Margerin, a member
of the Sacred College, left for Belgium with that intention; he was accompanied by Carnot, Dugied and
Pierre Leroux. The latter had now entirely given
in his adhesion to Saint-Simonism, which he con-

[32] ' Œuvres,' vol. iii. p. 74, note.

tinued for a time to profess. The apostles were soon after followed by Laurent, but their exertions were attended with some danger. The clergy at Brussels were violently opposed to the new religion, and they possessed more power than in Paris. Their indignation was aroused by an attempt which had been made to secure an unoccupied church for the exercise of the Saint-Simonian religion. The passion and prejudice of the mob were stimulated by a proceeding which was represented as an insult to their faith; they threatened to pillage and burn the house which was occupied by the disciples, and it was therefore considered more prudent to bend to the storm and retire to Liége. There they met with a more favourable reception; the rector of the University placed a lecture-hall at their disposal, and, notwithstanding some threats of opposition on the part of the clergy, the meeting took place. It was attended by about 1500 persons, chiefly *bourgeois* and students, and the effect produced by the eloquence of Laurent is stated to have been immense. Shortly afterwards Duveyrier arrived, and followed up this success by energetic measures at Louvain and Ghent. At Louvain the head of the College refused to allow him the use of a lecture-hall, and the hotel-keeper was equally determined that he should not address a meeting in any room in his house. But Duveyrier was not to be deterred by these difficulties; in the afternoon he proceeded outside the town, followed by a large number of students, and directed his steps to a wood in the vicinity, and there, under the shade of the trees, amid the calm of a summer day, the persecuted apostle declared his mission. The effect of his words was intensified by the beauty of the scene by which he was surrounded. The enthusiasm of his audience was kindled by his eloquence, and upon that day many disciples were added to the church. This energetic apostle also founded a newspaper at Brussels, called 'L'Organisateur Belge,' which flourished for six months. In the meantime, however, a severe opposition had arisen in France; it was first manifested at Versailles, where the weekly discourse had to be discontinued, to avoid creating a disturbance. Upon this occasion, however, the mob appear to have laboured under a misapprehension, for, with their accustomed penetration, they are said to have identified the Saint-Simonians with the Jesuits. No such mistake occurred at Paris, where the *préfet* ordered the Salle de la Redoute to be closed. It appears that an influential family had discovered that one of its members was infected with the new principles, and was accustomed to attend the Redoute. In order to remove the temptation, they enlisted a few workmen in their service, whom they paid to create a disturbance; these persons found the employment so congenial to their taste, that the proprietors of shops in the neigh-

bourhood were compelled to close their windows, and
alarm became general. These circumstances were
fully known to the mayor of the *arrondissement*, and
he communicated them to his superior, who, however,
prohibited the meeting instead of punishing the peace-
breakers. Wherever the doctrine penetrated it had to
encounter ignorant opposition, which was generally
excited by the leaders of the retrograde party. The
disciples had to resort to the expedient of choosing
their audience, so that the proceedings might not be
disturbed. The strangest rumours were circulated
about them. Some said they must be paid by Lafayette; others suggested Napoleon II.; others Henri
V.: some believed their proceedings were simply a
trap laid by the police; others suspected that the
Jesuits must be at the bottom of it. Yet neither the
danger the disciples had to encounter, nor the prejudice they had to surmount, could daunt their resolution; the work of conversion proceeded with ever-
increasing energy and success. Six departmental
churches were formed at Toulouse, Montpellier, Lyons,
Metz, Dijon, Limoges; besides these, there were centres of propagation in nine other towns in France.
They had established one church in Belgium and six
centres, while missionaries from Paris were continually
traversing the country in all directions, keeping alive
the enthusiasm of the local disciples, and daily gaining fresh converts. Among the most active were

1831.   Laurent, Duveyrier, Reynaud, Jules Lechevalier, and
Barrault. Jules Lechevalier addressed a large audience at Dijon, and a brother of the celebrated Père
Lacordaire was present. He described the effect produced by the preacher:—"The two or three friends
I have at Dijon are Saint-Simonians; no one talks
of anything else. Partly from curiosity, I went to
hear Lechevalier; the hall was filled to excess, and
the orator was listened to attentively. The manner
in which the audience was carried away, and the keen
sympathy excited amongst them, proved that some
merit must attach to a doctrine that can arouse so
much unexpected feeling among the spectators, and
so much devotion in the heart of the preacher. Twice
I heard the voice of the disciples of Saint-Simon, and
never will the recollection be effaced from my memory. The feeling aroused in my heart was one of
hatred and contempt towards my former life. But.
now I am happy, for the future opens before me full
of life and youth." At Tours Barrault achieved a
prodigious success. When he painted in glowing language the misery that affects the poor, he moved his
audience to tears, and struck them with shame as he
denounced their indifference. "A la vue de ce peuple
entier, que vous voyez dans la fange de vos rues et de
vos places, sur de misérables grabats, au milieu de
l'air fétide des caves et des greniers, dans des hôpi-
taux encombrés, dans des bagnes hideux, se mouvoir,

pâle de faim et de privations, exténué par un rude
travail, à moitié couvert de haillons, livré à des agita-
tions convulsives, dégoûtant d'immoralité, meurtri de
chaînes, vivant à peine—je vous adjure tous, enfants
des classes privilégiées, levez vous, et la main appuyée
sur ces plaies putrides et saignantes, enfants des
classes privilégiées, qui vous engraissez de la sueur de
cette classe misérable exploitée à votre profit, jurez
que vous n'avez aucune part à ses souffrances, à ses
douleurs, à son agonie. Jurez, vous ne l'oseriez pas !
. . . Oui je veux, marchant plus hardiment dans les
voies de l'apostolat, vous faire rougir, si je puis, de
votre endurcissement et de votre stérile pitié, attacher
comme un remords à vos âmes languissantes le sou-
venir de mes paroles : . . . ou plutôt je veux, je veux
vous exciter à venir, en mêlant vos larmes aux nôtres,
vous jeter dans les bras de la famille saint-simonienne, afin de trouver au milieu de nous ce que vous
chercheriez vainement ailleurs—la paix, l'amour, l'espérance et les premières douceurs de l'association universelle."[33] In truth, the Saint-Simonians had recently adopted measures with a view to exercise a
more direct influence upon the labouring classes;
they had begun by attracting about twenty workmen
on Sunday to the Rue Monsigny.[34] At first they
came alone, but after a time they brought along with
them their friends and relations, so that the numbers

[33] 'Œuvres,' vol. iii. pp. 232-3.   [34] Ib. vol. iv. p. 80.

1831. rapidly increased; it was then determined to take more decided steps to secure this class of converts, and to exercise supervision over them. Henry Fournel and Claire Bazard were placed at the head of the propaganda. In each of the twelve *arrondissements* of Paris a male and a female missionary were permanently established. A registry was opened, in which the name, residence, and occupation of each member were duly entered; they were divided into two classes, "the Faithful" and the "Catechumens," according to the progress they had made in the doctrine. The number of the former had reached (Sept. 1831) 220,[35] of whom nearly half were women; the number of the latter was from three to four hundred. To avoid confusion or interruption at the meetings, each member received a ticket, without which he was not permitted to be present. In addition to the missionaries, a doctor was attached to each *arrondissement*, to attend to the health of the converts and to vaccinate the children; they were assisted by two surgeons. Efforts were made still further to improve the condition of the poor by encouraging them to unite together, in order to derive benefit from association. Already, in two *arrondissements*, measures had been taken in this direction; upwards of 10,000 francs had been spent to procure two houses, situated in the Rue de la Tour

[35] These 220 workpeople belonged to fifty-four different occupations; the largest number were tailors (nineteen), printers or compositors (sixteen), shoemakers (ten).

d'Auvergne and the Rue Popincourt, where the workmen were to enjoy the advantages of board and lodg-
ing in common, besides instruction in the morals and
doctrine of the new faith.[36] " We have made new men
of these disciples from the old world," says Fournel,
in his report to Enfantin and Bazard. " They trusted
before to violence to ameliorate their condition, but
their faith is now in peace. They were disbelievers
because they appeared to have been abandoned by
God; now they recognize the messengers of God
himself in the men who surround them with the treasures of your love. They murmured against all authority, but they have learned to bless yours, in acknow-
ledging with pride that they have become your sons.
They were impatient for a rapid emancipation, but
they have now apprehended that it is only by long
efforts that that emancipation, peacefully acquired, can
be permanent." M. Gustave d'Eichthal was placed at
the head of the Industrial system, which it was proposed to attach to these establishments. It was intended to open a *workshop*, where the Saint-Simonians
would be employed, under the supervision of D'Eichthal, according to their capacity, and rewarded according to their work. Christianity, they said, has abân-
doned the poor to the charity of the rich; it has instructed them to pray day by day for their daily bread;
but Saint-Simon has come to terminate this anxiety

[36] ' Œuvres,' vol. iv. pp. 49, 65, 72.

K

1831. and misery. It is his desire that the poor shall obtain
and consume the bread they have justly merited by
their own labour. "Vous nous avez dit, plus d'ana-
thème sur la matière : plus de cendres ni de cilice, de
jeûne ni de macération : plus de vêtements poudreux,
de demeures étroites et sombres, et aussi plus d'esclavage, plus de servitude, plus de salaire ; mais à tous la
santé, la force, la richesse ; à tous les honneurs du
temple et les joies de l'association."[37]

Saint-Simonism had now developed into a large organization, and its expenses had increased in proportion.
For five years after the death of its founder its converts
were restricted to a very narrow circle of disciples;
they were chiefly recruited from the liberal professions
or from commerce, and their private resources were
sufficient to meet the requirements of the new faith.
But from the year 1830 the propaganda proceeded
upon an increasing scale : they acquired the ' Globe '
newspaper, which was very far from being commer-
cially prosperous, and they distributed vast numbers
of copies gratuitously; they hired a large hotel in
Paris, in the Rue Monsigny, besides the various halls

[37] ' Œuvres,' vol. iii. p. 212. Great distress had followed the Revolution of July, and Messrs. Crebassol and Rosier opened an *atelier
national*, in order to provide work to men who could not obtain it elsewhere. They appealed for subscriptions in a manner that conveyed a
menace to those who would refuse to contribute; and M. Michel Chevalier wrote to say that their proceedings were not connected in any
way with the Saint-Simonians. (*Ib.* vol. iv. pp. 21–25.)

used for their lectures; they dispatched expensive missions to Belgium, and to various districts in France; they inundated the country with volumes of exposi- tions and pamphlets, and finally they endeavoured to organize workmen into communities, and to employ them in industrial pursuits. Some of the members became so absorbed in the work they had thus under- taken, that they were obliged to resign their profes- sional employment, upon which they had hitherto subsisted, and they thus became a charge to the faith. Enfantin retired from his office in the Caisse Hypothé- caire; Hoart, who had attained the rank of captain in the artillery, resigned his commission. Many others acted similarly, though the most remarkable instance of self-sacrifice was that of Fournel. He not only gave up his appointment at Creuzot, and made large contributions to meet the expenses of the faith, but he also offered to lend a sum of 90,000 francs; he more- over promised to increase this loan by 120,000 or 150,000 francs as soon as he inherited his share in the family estate. His liberality was imitated by M. Gus- tave d'Eichthal, whose relations were rich bankers.

The other disciples acted in the same manner, ac- cording to their ability, and no less than 250,000 francs were collected from July, 1830, to July, 1831. Of this sum 100,000 francs were spent on the 'Globe,' 72,000 francs on maintaining the staff of functionaries con- nected with the administration, the direction of the

1831. workmen, the industrial undertakings, and the missionaries; and 16,000 francs were expended on the mission to Belgium and elsewhere. Besides this sum of 250,000 francs, the large amount of 600,000 francs had been subscribed in property which had not yet been realized. It is not to be supposed, however, that these numbers represent actual gifts to the association: a large portion of the money had been lent by disciples whose faith exceeded their prudence, and who believed that the capital would be judiciously invested, and the interest regularly paid, for they fancied that the establishment of a manufactory upon Saint-Simonian principles would be a safe and profitable undertaking.

While the society was thus outwardly prosperous, another fierce controversy had arisen within the precincts of the Sacred College, which led at the close of the year to the secession of M. Bazard. Although women were highly favoured by the doctrines of Saint-Simon, they held aloof from the movement. Madame Bazard continued for a long time to be the single female disciple. At length, in 1829, she was joined by three or four others, the wives and sisters of leading converts. Special lectures were delivered with the view of attracting others, and the most eloquent speakers were selected for the undertaking. These efforts were in some degree successful, and Madame Bazard was appointed to maintain discipline among the converts of her own sex ; she found the task far from easy. " La hiérarchie pour nous," she says in 1831, " est un vain mot, elle ne porte aucun fruit. Nos réunions se passent dans le tumulte et le désordre ; c'est un chaos dans lequel il serait impossible de reconnaître les inférieures de la supérieure, car la mère ne sait imposer le respect aux enfants, les enfants ne savent point se soumettre à la mère."[38] Madame Fournel was the next lady of consequence after Madame Bazard, and they both had seats in the Sacred College. That body was then occupied chiefly with the marriage system, and the subject gave rise to the most extraordinary excitement. Scarcely a year had elapsed since Bazard-Enfantin had issued a declaration in reply to an accusation made by M. Dupin in the Chambre des Députés. M. Dupin had charged the Saint-Simonians with advocating community of property and promiscuous intercourse. They had explicitly denied both of these charges ; as regards the latter, they explained the exact position they maintained with reference to women. " They demand that one man be united to one woman, but they teach that the wife should become the equal of her husband, and be associated with him in the exercise of the triple function of the temple, the State, and the family ; so that the ' social individual,' which has hitherto been the *man* alone, may henceforward be composed of man and woman. The Saint-Simonian

[38] ' Œuvres,' vol. iii. p. 116.

religion proposes only to terminate the shameful traffic, the legal prostitution, which, under the name of marriage, now so frequently sanctifies a monstrous union between devotion and egotism, education and ignorance, youth and decrepitude."[39]　At the same time it maintains the inviolability of the union. This declaration reflected the opinions of Bazard more faithfully than those of Enfantin. According to the latter, persons of different temperaments should not be controlled by the same law. Let those whose affections are constant adhere to one companion throughout life; but it is not desirable to impose such an obligation universally—on the contrary, it is highly necessary, in order to secure the happiness of those who are naturally disposed to change, to legitimitize successive unions with different persons.[40] Enfantin made known his views in letters and conversation, till at length they were brought before the disciples. They then gave rise to the most heated debates; some became ardent partisans of Enfantin, others retained the opinions of

---

[39] 'Œuvres,' vol. iv. p. 124.

[40] At a later period Enfantin remarked with energy, "Dans ces mariages sataniques consacrés devant l'Église, où le prêtre vient ajouter, au poids de la chaîne qu'il forge, ces mots terribles, fidélité, éternité, l'un des époux marche souvent au sacrifice, au vrai sacrifice chrétien, à la mortification de la chair, au plus horrible supplice, à la plus hideuse croix, et pourtant la conscience du prêtre est pure, s'il croit que les deux époux ont la foi, car il s'inquiète peu alors des douleurs que l'un des deux pourra souffrir dans sa chair; c'est une visite de Dieu, une bénédiction du Seigneur, une épreuve."—*Ib.* vol. xvi. p. 58.

their youth with violent tenacity. At times the discussion would be continued day and night without intermission. The youths, who were more excitable and less able to support fatigue, overcome by faintness were borne unconscious from the room; yet the fiery debate proceeded without an instant's pause. Occasionally the reason of a member suffered from the intolerable excitement: one fell into a trance and fancied he had received the gift of prophecy; another, seized with convulsions, imagined that he was possessed by the Holy Spirit. Such scenes, it has been said, have had no parallel since the history of the Anabaptists. Enfantin alone retained his calm throughout the whole discussion. It occasionally descended into personalities, and Bazard even reproached Enfantin with immorality; this accusation created much scandal, and gave rise to a declaration on the part of Rodrigue that Enfantin was "l'homme le plus moral de mon temps."[41] In truth the question which originally had been purely speculative had at length become, according to the admission of M. Chevalier, nothing more than a struggle for supremacy between MM. Bazard and Enfantin. Although very many of the members disagreed from the latter, they were not the less determined to retain him as their leader. It was at length decided that Enfantin should be declared the supreme head of the New Faith, and that Bazard and Rodrigue should occupy a posi-

[41] 'Œuvres,' vol. iv. p. 201.

tion of equal dignity to one another immediately below him. Bazard was induced at first to accept this resolution; but the day after he altered his decision, and finally withdrew. He was followed by his wife, M. and Mme. Fournel, Pierre Leroux, Jules Lechevalier, Carnot, Cazeaux, and by many others. These unfortunate disputes were the cause of much misery. Jules Lechevalier doubtless expressed the feelings of many besides himself when he acknowledged that he was in a pitiable condition. " I doubt," he said, " I doubt even of Saint-Simon, I doubt of those who have continued his work, I doubt of everything,—in fact I become once more a sceptic." Another disciple confessed " Je suis seul, je cherche ma doctrine ;" to which Enfantin characteristically replied, " C'est de toutes les positions la plus pénible."[42]

The divisions with which the Sacred College had been convulsed ever since its foundation were attributed to the absence of independent action on the part of women. It was thought that so soon as they entered into complete association, and upon the same equality with men, all division must necessarily terminate. The result, therefore, of the recent dissension must have been eminently unsatisfactory, for not a single woman continued in the hierarchy along with Enfantin; yet it was necessary, according to his theory, to complete the likeness upon earth to the androgynous deity

[42] 'Œuvres,' vol. iv. p. 195.

·1881.

above, and till that was achieved no important success could be expected, either as regards the evolution of doctrine or the reorganization of society. Accordingly, by the side of Enfantin, who was now styled Père Suprême, the empty chair of Bazard was retained as the symbol of the appeal that was made to woman. It was believed that a female Messiah would arise, and reveal her mission by the exalted doctrine she would announce; her place would be by the side of Enfantin, and her advent would be the signal of the final accomplishment of the emancipation of her sex.[43] Till this august apparition takes place, no woman will be permitted in future to take part in the proceedings of the society.[44] According to a statement of Bazard, the members of the Sacred College were unanimous in their opposition to Enfantin; yet such was the influence he exercised that he was able to overcome all difficulties, and to secure the supreme direction of affairs to himself. At the same time he did not impose his views

---

[43] " Nous espérons tous la venue d'une femme, Messie de son sexe, qui doit sauver le monde de la prostitution, comme Jésus le délivra de l'esclavage. De cette femme Messie, je sens que je suis le Précurseur; pour elle je suis ce que saint Jean fut pour Jésus; là est toute ma vie, là est le lieu de tous mes actes."—*Œuvres*, vol. viii. p. 54.

[44] " Les femmes n'apparaîtront plus sur l'estrade, à la prédication; Elles seront, extérieurement, toutes à l'état d'appel, comme toutes les femmes du monde qui nous entourent " (pointing to the vacant chair). " Voici le symbole de cet appel; ce sera le seul qui manifestera l'appel de la femme aux yeux de tous. La femme manque à la doctrine, elle ne s'y est pas révélée, elle est encore à l'état d'esclavage."—*Ib.* vol. iv. p. 198.

1831. as a matter of necessity upon his disciples, and some
remained who differed profoundly from him upon this
vital question.   The dispute agitated the provinces,
and the faith of many became lukewarm.   The zealous
bishop of the south, Rességuier, remained in a neutral
condition, unable to keep pace with the rapid development the doctrine had undergone ; the church of Toulouse was reduced to four members, and that of Metz
was reported to be completely disorganized.   Lamoricière reports the consternation created in the " church
of Africa" when it learned that discord had arisen in
the " temple of peace ;" but his own faith remained
unshaken, and his devotion to the cause was greatly
to its advantage.   " Je suis si profondément convaincu
de la vérité de la doctrine," he wrote to D'Eichthal,
" que je m'écrierais comme Galilée ' Dieu fera la grâce
qu'on résoudra l'objection.' "[45]   Captain Lefranc describes him then as " plein de jeunesse, de chaleur,
d'enthousiasme, d'une foi vive, ardente, entraînée, animée—le vieux partisan de Condillac, d'Holbach et de
Helvétius, relevé naguère par Cousin, T. Jouffroy et
Damiron, de la fange du matérialisme—il trouve dans
la religion nouvelle cette autorité dont il sent profondément le besoin, et un aliment à cet amour qui fut
toujours pour son cœur le premier des biens."[46]   Many
years afterwards, when his fame as a general was established, and the fervour of his youth had passed, he

[45] ' Œuvres,' vol. v. p. 62.   [46] Ib. vol. v. p. 68.

lost his reverence for the religion he had recently em-   1831.
braced, and treated the Père Suprême with considerable
coolness.   Shortly after the secession of Bazard, other
eminent members found a pretext for withdrawing
from the school; among these were Laurent and
Transon, who subsequently became converts to the
system of Fourier.   But by far the most serious loss
the faith had sustained was in Bazard, the leader of the
revolt.   Enfantin obtained his influence by the charm
of his character, and the admiration with which he inspired his followers.   Bazard maintained his authority
by the force of his will and the energy that characterized his conduct.   At the outset of the movement
his co-operation was invaluable, when many heteroge-
neous elements had to be combined, and many independent and antagonistic natures harmonized and governed,
and before they had fallen under the spell subsequently
exercised by Enfantin.   His influence was likewise felt
in moderating the hardy speculations of his colleague,
who when freed from this restraint ran into the wildest
extravagance both of opinion and of conduct.   Bazard
did not long survive the separation; he died in the
following summer, and his funeral afforded Enfantin
an opportunity for exhibiting some of the best and
some of the most grotesque sides of his character.

With few exceptions, those who, like Bazard, withdrew from Enfantin, did not on that account forsake
the Saint-Simonian faith, as it has been explained at

1831. the beginning of this chapter. The disciples appear, however, to have abandoned the fantastic materialism of an androgynous Deity, and to have embraced the sublime faith of the Pantheist, who acknowledges the unity of God and Nature, and who worships His majesty and tenderness in the manifold forms of Her grandeur and beauty. The seceders, not less than the followers of Enfantin, maintained that mind and matter are equally sacred, that manual and intellectual labour are of a religious nature, and that politics should form a part of religion; that woman is the equal of man; that the aim of all social institutions should be the moral, intellectual, and physical amelioration of the greatest number; that nations gravitate providentially towards universal association; that modern society passes more and more from the state of war to that of peace, from destruction to production, from military to industrial ascendancy; and that in this new society every one will be classed according to his capacity, and rewarded according to his works. But to this intelligible creed, Enfantin imposed upon his immediate followers other tenets that demanded a larger faith. He taught that, from time to time, a revelation is made to man by a prophet, who is gifted with extraordinary and supernatural wisdom. Such were Moses and Christ, such is Saint-Simon.[47] The two first reve-

47 " La LOI VIVANTE ne se trouve qu'aux époques organiques, et alors la LOI c'est l'HOMME; toujours elle a un NOM et ce nom est celui de SON

1831.

lations are abrogated by the latter, which is final, inasmuch as it is the "revelation of progress." The former had each its sacred book, so also has Saint-Simonism, which was begun by its founder, and is even now being continued by Enfantin and his disciples. Unlike the canon of the Old and New Testaments, however, the written law of the new faith will never close till the destinies of humanity shall have been accomplished. This circumstance is overlooked by those who accuse Enfantin of promulgating doctrines for which no authority can be found in the writings of his master. They forget that his doctrine is not stereotyped in his works, but it has become incarnate in the association of men who perpetuate his name; upon them has devolved the authority of continuing and developing the mission of Saint-Simon, and they have recognised in Enfantin the supreme head of the Church. His words have now become a living law to his followers, who are bound to accept whatever he announces with the implicit faith accorded by a Jew to Moses, or by a Christian to the lawgiver of Galilee. Hence the apostles of Saint-Simonism sought to restore the sentiment of authority which they complained had long since receded before the growing love of liberty.[48] They encouraged the

AUTEUR; et d'abord celle qui domine toutes les autres, celle qui a fondé la société, c'est, selon les temps, ou la loi de Numa, ou celle de Moïse, ou celle de Christ, comme dans l'avenir ce sera celle de SAINT-SIMON."— *Œuvres*, vol. xiv. p. 110.

[48] "It would be impossible, they said, indeed, to renew obedience,

1831.   disciples to look to their 'Father' with a childlike confidence, as alone competent to solve all the difficulties
by which they are beset. "Dear children," writes
Enfantin, " do not grieve him who gives his life for you;
think of him; come to him if you doubt of the morality
of your thoughts or your deeds; his presence, or the
recollection of him, will impart calm to you; have confidence in him; if he deceives himself as to your future,
it is still from him that you will find that which his
imperfect foresight was not at first able to discover.
He is the living law which God has given you for your
guidance, he inspires you. Do you not feel that his
love for you is a powerful condition of his morality? so
also, the love which you have for him will be a powerful guarantee of yours."[49] As has been already explained, the Father is, just at present, peculiarly liable
to error, because of the absence of the female Messiah,
who should be by his side, and influence all his decisions.
To the sacerdotal couple every disciple will open his
heart, he will confide implicitly in them, he will reveal
to them the mysteries of his thoughts and the details

either to Cæsarism or to Catholicism, but if we substitute the power of
love for the power of mere physical force, or the power of artful
duplicity, we shall be able to excite once more in the heart of man a
sentiment of which it has been long deprived, and which slumbers, that
of gratitude on the part of the feeble, to the strong who protect them;
of the ignorant, to the wisdom of those who enlighten them; of every
living being, to those who kindle a flame in their heart."—*Œuvres*,
vol. xiv. p. 88.

[49] 'Œuvres,' vol. xiv. p. 132.

of his acts, the pleasures and pains that afflict his body and soul, because the priesthood is man and woman, the father and mother of all, and its paternal and maternal love inspires the son as well as the daughter with faith.[50] The sacerdotal couple will have other arduous duties to perform besides that of confessors and directors of their sheep.

It has been already remarked that the new Christianity contemplated the pleasures of the world from a totally different point of view to that occupied by the exponents of the old. "Sanctifiez-vous," exhorted Bazard, " dans le travail et dans le plaisir."   It was a maxim of the new faith that the flesh is of equal dignity and sanctity to the mind, and that it is no more reprehensible to indulge the one than the other. What they termed the " Réhabilitation de la Chair " became a grand object with the Saint-Simonian teachers, as its mortification had been among the Christians. It was not alone that the natural passions should have full scope for healthy action, but the senses should be gratified by all the resources of art and science, and material prosperity. The theories that would turn the world into a valley of tears were contemptuously discarded, and the opposite view, of the dignity and religious character of labour, as the means of conquering nature in order to satisfy human desires, was strenuously inculcated. To guide mankind towards material prosperity was to be a part

[50] ' Œuvres', vol. xiv. p. 157.

1831. of the sacerdotal functions, for the enjoyment of earth, not less than of heaven, is the object of the new religion. It will, therefore, be the duty of the androgynous priests of the future to develope science and industry, and to summon the beauties of art to arrest the attention of the masses.

But as the sensual passions, even of a comparatively gross form, are not reprobated by the new faith, it will also form a part of their duty to charm by their personal beauty those of their flock who are susceptible to such influence. "The priest and priestess exercise their office with all the powers of their intelligence, and also with their beauty, because the priests of the future do not mortify their flesh like the Christians, they do not veil their faces, they do not cover themselves with ashes, they do not punish themselves with stripes, they are beautiful as well as wise—they are good."[51] They recognize all the grace of modesty, but likewise do not forget the charm of voluptuousness. A world that has been perverted by austerity can hardly conceive the power that beauty is destined to exercise in the future. A faint notion may be gleaned from the history of chivalry, where the smile of a mistress is found to have been sufficient to excite to the most daring acts of heroism.[52] Such

[51] 'Œuvres,' vol. xiv. p. 157.
[52] Speaking of the clergy of the middle ages, Enfantin says, "A côté de ce sacerdoce mâle, il y avait un rêve d'avenir, la chevalerie, puissante tradition du passé, pour l'homme, mais inspiration, prophétie,

were among the new principles to which Enfantin invited the attention of his followers. They were required to believe that he, Enfantin, was the Living Law of God. At first he was but the successor to Saint-Simon, but after a while the master paled before the increasing brightness of the disciple, and Saint-Simon dwindled into a John the Baptist, while Enfantin stood forth as the central figure in the picture, the supreme prophet of the new faith. In order to explain this position and the consequences that must result from its acceptance, meetings were held twice a week in the Rue Monsigny, by the disciples who still remained faithful after the secession of Bazard. Enfantin speedily assumed his sacerdotal functions, and submitted each of his followers to a very strict examination as regards both their conduct and opinions. He fancied that when they had obtained a clear revelation of the different characters which, as he piously put it, God had assembled to form a family of apostles, they would at the same time have secured a know-

révélation d'avenir pour la femme. Ici la femme s'initia, pour ainsi dire, à la maternité du sacerdoce futur ; alors elle exerçait un empire moral immense sur de jeunes cœurs qui Chrétiens, mais non clercs, avaient bien en eux le saint amour d'un Dieu pur esprit, mais qui brûlaient aussi du désir de plaire. Le chevalier, le page, invoquait Dieu et sa dame ; et sa dame avait pour lui le divin caractère de la femme chrétienne, de la Vierge, mais pourtant c'était une femme ; et lorsque dans son église sombre le clerc ne pouvait charmer son cœur brûlant qu'avec un rêve mystique d'amour, la loi vivante d'amour était, hors de l'église, reine dans les tournois, *châtelaine* respectée, bénie, adorée, c'était la dame."—*Œuvres*, vol. xvi. p. 47.

L

ledge of the various characters that exist in the world, and whose types were to be found providentially within their own circle. Nearly a volume of the 'Œuvres' is filled with autobiographies and confessions of a singularly curious character, and as some of the persons who thus imparted their confidences to Enfantin are still living and occupied high positions under the Empire, it must be far from gratifying to them to find the seals. of confession so unceremoniously broken.

Gustave d'Eichthal explained how he had been born a Jew and passed finally into Saint-Simonism, having traversed many religious phases. His faith in Enfantin knew no bounds: " I believe in God," he cried, " I believe in Saint-Simon, and I believe that Saint-Simon is in you." " You have said well," answered Enfantin, " I do not ask for more." [53] " Now we know," he said to a friend, " the manner of man who is amongst us. To him it is given to root up and to destroy, to build and to plant; in him all human life has its development and progress; in him are peace, riches, science, —the future of the world. We know it, and it is this knowledge that gives us strength. The world does not know it, and it is that which constitutes its weakness." [54] He describes how, overcome by fatigue, he had fallen into a trance, and was transported in imagination to the Cathedral of Notre Dame. Once more

[53] 'Œuvres,' vol. vi. p. 5.   [54] Ib. vol. vi. p. 163.

the sacred music of the Mass fell upon his ear; once more he knelt before the altar and partook of the flesh of the Christian God. The love he had felt in bygone years rekindled in his heart with its former passion; the Master whom he had adored stood before him in the flesh, and he recognized him in the form of Enfantin. "Oui, Père," he exclaimed, "ce Jésus que j'ai si ardemment aimé, maintenant je le sens en toi." [55]

Barrault, possessed by a similar enthusiasm, declared, "Father, you are to me the living law of humanity,— imperfect, no doubt, because that chair, the symbol of our hopes, is vacant; but yet I assert, and my brow bears no mark of servility, that I adore in you the highest manifestation of God in humanity." [56] "Father," he said upon another occasion, "You are the Messiah of God and the king of nations. Jerusalem saw its Christ and knew him not; Paris has seen your face and heard your voice. France only knows your name." [57]

M. Lambert has given us a touching picture of his life at college and the mental struggles by which he was harassed. He devoted himself to science and philosophy, and they led him to despair; the deepest problems of humanity were continually present to his mind. "Fatality or Providence?" such was the awful question to be resolved; it haunted

[55] 'Œuvres,' vol. vi. p. 187. [56] Ib. vol. v. p. 19. [57] Ib. vol. vi. p. 197.

1831. him by day and deprived him of rest by night. At length Transon, a Saint-Simonian apostle, saved him from the precipice and restored him to life. He restored him in the name of Enfantin and in that of Saint-Simon, whom he represented as prophets, bearing to men the rule of their lives. He explained how the world was not divided by two antagonistic principles, eternally destined to conflict, how humanity progressed unceasingly through the ages to a continuously more prosperous condition, how the universe is submitted to a law of harmony, and how God makes himself felt in that universal harmony.[58] Then did the convert determine .to devote his life to carry the gospel that had saved him to others who were still in the darkness from which he had happily emerged. Another disciple makes a similar confession; till the new religion saved him he was a republican in politics; in morality he denied all law; in religion he was an atheist,—he believed in nothing, not even in love, which he regarded as a weakness. Very different from this was the condition to which Raymond Bonheur, the father of the great artist, confessed. " I devoted," he said, " all my life to loving women; I loved them as an artist; it is for their sake that I am forced to speak and act. I desire to be near them, for they know I love them; and I find myself nobler, greater, and better when I am permitted to touch them." It was highly agreeable to discover a religion that en-

[58] ' Œuvres,' vol. xv. p. 62.

couraged rather than restrained these amorous tendencies ; and, accordingly, the gratitude of Bonheur to Enfantin is boundless. "Father," he says, "I believe in you as I believe in the sun. You are to my eyes the sun of humanity; you warm it with your love, the living image of the infinite love of God." [59] A well-known political economist, who was among the most ardent disciples, has given us some amusing traits of his youth. At college his masters were accustomed to observe what an insolent little fellow he was. He retained, he says, that character to a later period, and no doubt he has found it useful in his subsequent career. He remarks, as a curious instance of modesty, that up to fifteen years of age he had never once dreamed of ever being a king, though he often fancied himself a minister of the crown. He thought a minister of public instruction would be but a poor affair, something like an upper schoolmaster, but that it would be fine indeed to be minister of foreign affairs, and to wear a grand dress and receive all the great people of other nations ; he would like to have been the chief of Napoleon's staff, because that imposing functionary was always surrounded by aides-de-camp mounted on fine horses, and wore a grander dress than the Emperor himself. But a year ago he complains that he was still living in the outer darkness of a family according to the flesh. He was suffering and

[59] 'Œuvres,' vol. xv. p. 218.

1831. ill at ease; he was languishing beneath a business
the world had imposed upon him, and which oppressed
him precisely because it was too trivial. But Enfantin
summoned him to the good work; he gave him back
health, faith, and love. From that time the veneration
of the disciple increased, because his master has ever
appeared to him great, strong, and full of goodness. At
times indeed his faith was sorely tried, though he never
went so far as to doubt. At first he protested against the
ethical theories that were propounded. He denounced
them as monstrous, immoral, and disgusting; but as
time went on his opinion changed, his difficulties disappeared, till at length he has been led to see that the
new relation between the sexes is the highest law that
has ever been promulgated—it is big with large results and destined to terminate the miseries that
oppress humanity. All this is told us with great
gravity, accompanied by a highly profound psycho-
logical analysis. Among the disciples there was considerable unanimity of opinion, but yet much personal jealousy and antagonism. In their confessions they often expressed themselves with painful
candour, both as respected themselves and others;
but the influence of Enfantin was supreme, and
in his presence their differences were harmonized,
and men rushed into one another's arms, imploring
and granting reconciliation. D'Eichthal, who was excessively excitable, was the most subject to these

seizures, and he was perpetually throwing his arms round the necks of the other disciples. It might be thought that Enfantin would have sought to moderate an excitement that so nearly approached to madness; and upon one occasion, indeed, he found it necessary to assure his disciples that "nul de nous n'est Dieu. Je suis un homme." But short of this he gave every encouragement to the most exaggerated opinions. He explained the defection of Bazard and others to have proceeded from their being void of religious sentiment. Their gross intelligence could never apprehend who Enfantin was; they were unwilling to recollect that the will of God is manifested from time to time through authorized human channels, and they failed to perceive that Enfantin was one of these. For the mission of conversion to which they were to devote their lives, the disciples were exhorted to keep their hearts full of faith, they must believe that God was not deceived when, after the death of Saint-Simon, he committed the destinies of the world into the hands of their master, Enfantin. We are assured that to the principal apostles he appeared not only as continuing the mission of Christ, "but as Christ himself, in all his divine grandeur, humanly developed through the course of ages." Duveyrier attests his conviction that a new life for the people has appeared in the capital of France, in that Divine Life, which has come to establish the religion of labour and joy. It has appeared under

the form of a young man, more beautiful and more holy than any other; it shines upon his brow, in his countenance, and in the sweetness of his smile; it has fallen with his words into the hearts of those who have listened to him. The people who approach him feel the contact of a palpable and visible God; they exclaim, " O God ! shall we have no part in the new life which you diffuse in the world ?" [60] Baud declared, "Father, you are for me the living law; I have faith in your promise. You are not God—you have said so yourself, and I feel it; but you are to me of all men the one who best knows the thoughts of God, and who has the most courage and constancy to work out the future you have announced to mankind." [61]

The meetings in which these curious scenes took place were held from the period of the separation of Bazard in November, 1831, to the middle of February in the following year. While the elder disciples thus sought to strengthen their faith, and to stimulate their enthusiasm, Rodrigue and Flachat conducted a mission to the labouring classes with a similar object. Men are occasionally deluded by the hope of a fresh start in life; it seems to them, for a moment, as though they could break completely with the past, throw aside their indolence and vice, put on a new character as they would a new coat, and forgetting the wretchedness and disappointments they have traversed, have

[60] 'Œuvres,' vol. vi. p. 174.   [61] Ib. vol. xv. p. 43.

courage to begin the world anew. But alas for these
brilliant hopes, there can be no break in the continuity
of existence, no second birth into a new life ; and the
errors and misfortunes of youth will extend their
shadow to the last dark hour. It is painful to read
the wild language of these ignorant men, who fancied
they had found in Enfantin a prophet of heaven, a
messenger of prosperity and happiness, who, by the
magic of his power, could make them new men in a
new world. The very lowest classes fell victims to
the enthusiasm; even a beggar who had gone about
in rags from door to door became a Saint-Simonian
convert and an energetic orator. But the exigencies
of the faith required that an appeal should be made
not the less to a different class; the apostles were
exhorted to be more particular as to the quality than
the number of the disciples they made. It was complained that of 400 persons whose names had been
recently registered, not more than 100 attended the
meetings, and only 10 were willing to unite themselves without reservation to the sect. Very many fell
away so soon as they were applied to for money to
assist the work. It was desired that an appeal should
be made at the outset to the generosity of a convert,
for in that way only could it be judged what manner
of man he was. It is true that such "exalted candour," such "noble apostolic insolence," might deter
many from joining, but their loss would be rather to

the advantage of the faith. Those who withstood this test were encouraged to continue in their professions or trades, as by so doing they could render more effectual assistance. Many of the early disciples had been carried away by too ardent an enthusiasm; they had completely abandoned the ordinary vocations of life, and had devoted themselves exclusively to preaching the new doctrine in language which was very grandiloquent, but often obscure. M. Lafitte had wittily remarked to these persons, "You post your advertisements too high; one cannot read them." It was now sought to rectify this error by adopting a clearer style, and entering into more intimate association with the rest of mankind.

In reviewing what had already been accomplished there was much room for congratulation, and much also for disappointment. The speculative tenets of the sect had indeed been widely diffused; they had penetrated Belgium, and every important town in France had a centre of propagation. But nothing had as yet been effected towards the introduction of industrial prosperity, or the classification of men according to their capacity. A few poor labourers had been recruited, from among those who are always ready to join any projected association, but no work had yet been got for them to do; they were in the receipt of charity, they were not organized for industrial enterprise. Yet even this condition afforded a proof to the world of the philanthropic

intentions with which the disciples of the new religion
were inspired; but it would be a mistake to imagine
that their ambition could be circumscribed within such
narrow limits. They contemplated the ultimate formation of a pacific army of labourers, led by distinguished scientific scholars, who would be the priests
of a new religion—of a religion that claimed the possession of the earth as the inheritance of the faithful,
and inculcated the development of its resources and
the enjoyment of its pleasures as a religious duty.
Unhappily, however, for the success of their enterprise, the Sacred College continued to be convulsed
by the division of its members, and in February
1832 Olinde Rodrigue, the eldest disciple, withdrew
from Enfantin, and proclaimed himself to be the true
representative of Saint-Simon. The cause of his separation was the view the Père Suprême entertained
respecting women, which daily became more and more
remarkable. Rodrigue was ready to admit great freedom for divorce in the event of ill-assorted unions,
and to afford every facility for the formation of new
engagements; but this was not sufficient to satisfy
Enfantin. He denied that he advocated promiscuous
relations, but, with every desire to be impartial, it is
not easy to acquit him of the charge. He held that
the woman only should be required to decide as to the
paternity of a child; he contemplated a state of society
in which no man would be able to form any opinion

upon so difficult a subject.[62] It may be fairly inferred
from this that the husband, if such a word is applicable, will have no right to exact fidelity from his
partner; and, to remove the embarrassment that would
naturally arise from such a state of affairs, the child
was to be separated from its parents as soon after
birth as was practicable, and become from that moment a charge to the State.[63]

For two months the contest between Rodrigue and
Enfantin raged with unabated vigour, and then at
length the intimate association that had lasted for six
years was dissolved, and the disputants had recourse
to fierce recriminations. Enfantin wrote a pastoral
letter to the churches in the provinces, in which he
explains how his religious thought had been fettered
for months past, first by Bazard and then by Rodrigue. It is a source of congratulation, he says, that
he is at length freed from their opposition. It was
inevitable that the new religion should find itself at

[62] "J'ai affirmé que, dans la famille saint-simonienne tout enfant devait pouvoir connaître son père. Enfantin a exprimé le vœu que la femme
seule fût appelée à s'expliquer sur cette grave question. Il a donc admis
des cas de promiscuité religieuse, tandis que j'ai seulement admis la
sanction du divorce et la sanctification des secondes noces."—*Manifesto
of Rodrigue*, vol. v. p. 241.

[63] "'Logiciens impitoyables !' cried Rodrigue; 'vous vouliez enseigner
au nom de Saint-Simon qu'à l'avenir l'enfant, vagissant à peine, serait
arraché au regard même de sa mère délivrée, aussi bien qu'à celui du
père, pour abolir plus sûrement, selon vous, tous les priviléges de la
naissance.' "—*Ib*. vol. vi. p. 43.

Bazard shared this opinion with Enfantin. (*Ib*. vol. xiv. p. 191.)

issue with the Christian teaching, which subordinates the woman to the man, and with the Jewish system, where the family is so important an element in the State. The Christian has finally protested in Bazard, and now the Jew in Rodrigue. Bazard replied that although he knew the word ' Christian' was a term of reproach in the mouth of Enfantin, and scarcely applicable in the present case, yet he accepted it without indignation. He says that at all periods of dissolution disorder produces two very different results, one in the way of evil, the other in that of good. The first systematizes, organizes, and sanctifies every vice; the other separates from them the germs of the future, the progressive tendencies of the ages, exhibits them to the world, renders them attractive, and forms in that manner the new order that has become necessary. Enfantin and his disciples, unknown to themselves, are the organized missionaries of the evil tendencies, and it is well that they should be told so candidly.

Rodrigue took care to remark that his separation from Enfantin had in no degree united him to Bazard. The first was as naturally disposed to destructiveness in morality as the other to destructiveness in politics; they were both the last great representatives of the genius of revolution, which is at length tired of its own work, and will shortly give place to the more difficult task of reconstruction. Neither had ever

drawn from the vivifying source of the prophet.
Neither were ever kindled by the sacred fire, which for
the salvation of the world shone like a beacon amid
the fearful though sublime tempest raised by the
apostles of destruction. They might make their influence felt upon undisciplined minds diseased and exhausted by scepticism, they might make devotees or
fanatics, but religious men, never. The Enfantinists
are blinded by a senseless worship and a sensual
timidity; their conspiracy against morality, notwithstanding the ability and devotion that have been pro-
stituted in its service, will never attain success. It was
in vain that Enfantin sought to recall the erring
apostle; in vain he reminded him of the declaration
he had recently made that the Supreme Father was
the most moral of men, and that since the Sermon
on the Mount humanity had heard nothing so sublime
as the words that had fallen from his lips.·

Internal dissension was not the only misfortune produced by the peculiar opinions of Enfantin; the Government resolved to prosecute the association for inculcat-
ing doctrines that were subversive of public morality.
In the previous year Bazard, Michel Chevalier, Jules Lechevalier, and Cazeaux had suffered twenty-four hours'
imprisonment for having refused to serve in the National
Guard. They justified their conduct upon the grounds
that as they were ministers of a religion they were
exempted by law; the excuse was not, however, ac-

cepted, and they underwent punishment. But the
proceedings against them were now of a more serious
character. On Sunday the 23rd of January, just as
Enfantin, accompanied by some of his disciples, were
leaving their house in the Rue Monsigny to proceed
to the Salle Taitbout, to take part in the religious instruction of their flock, they were met by a detach-
ment of the Municipal Guard under the command of
a Commissary of Police. They were at once made
close prisoners, and prevented from holding any communication with the public outside. The Municipal
Guard was soon after reinforced by a piquet of grena-
diers of the National Guard, by a company of Voltigeurs
of the 52nd Regiment of the Line, and by a squadron
of hussars. Simultaneously with this military demonstration, another of an equally imposing character
took place before the Salle Taitbout. The hall was
already occupied by the disciples, who were listening
to the impassioned eloquence of Barrault. Their proceedings were interrupted by the entry of the public
prosecutor, accompanied by a magistrate, and supported
by regular troops of the line, and the municipal guard.
The greatest confusion at once ensued. The magistrate,
by virtue of the 291st article of the " Code Pénal,"
summoned the meeting to dissolve. The order was
received with tumultuous disapprobation, but the voice
of Barrault was heard above the angry murmur of the
crowd. " You come," he said, " you come here to

1832. seek a gospel of peace; prove yourselves now to be pacific. Preserve your calm, and retire with tranquillity."

The order was at once obeyed, the hall was cleared, and the magistrate formally closed it and affixed his seal to the door. In the meanwhile, in the Rue Monsigny the Saint-Simonians had recovered from their surprise, and sought to turn the occasion to the advantage of the faith. They accordingly commenced to preach to the astonished soldiers by whom they were surrounded, they distributed tracts with the zeal of evangelists, and made every effort to ensure their conversion. We are told that these labours were not in vain. Many who till that day were prejudiced against the sect were reconciled by the peaceful attitude of the disciples, and learned to regard with admiration the doctrines they had heretofore only heard of to ridicule or abhor. They had heard that the Saint-Simonians were opposed to the existence of property; they were surprised to find among them men who like Baud, Alexis Petit, and D'Eichthal were the heirs to considerable fortunes. But the attitude of Enfantin was, we are informed, peculiarly imposing; he was surrounded by an atmosphere of calm and dignity which he communicated to all who approached him. The government functionaries, who had triumphantly closed the Salle Taitbout, at length arrived at the Rue Monsigny. They were, we are told, especially affected by the impressive manner of

Enfantin, but notwithstanding they gathered strength to proceed with the execution of their duty. They commenced a diligent search for the papers of the sect, which they continued for three hours; then having summoned Enfantin and Rodrigue to appear before them next day, they retired with the account books, correspondence, and any other documents upon which they thought it possible to sustain a criminal charge.

After the retreat of Bazard and his followers, Olinde Rodrigue had undertaken the mission to workmen which had been hitherto intrusted to M. Fournel. In order that it might be conducted upon a more extended scale, he determined to form a " Financial Association," with a view to raise capital from the wealthy and unemployed classes. It was proposed in the first place to establish elementary schools, where the children of disciples might be educated together without reference to the rank or fortune of their parents; secondly, to found industrial and agricultural associations, by which the evils of competition might be finally abolished ; and thirdly, to organize a missionary system for the propagation of the faith by means of books and pamphlets, to be distributed gratuitously, and also by the advocacy of paid lecturers. The security that was offered to the shareholders in this company was the subscriptions and voluntary offerings of the Saint-Simonians and their future converts, and whatever profit might be derived from the associations

M

that were contemplated. When therefore Enfantin and Rodrigue appeared before the magistrate, they found that they had to encounter some formidable charges. They were accused of having raised money upon a wholly fictitious security; they were accused of having held meetings of more than twenty persons without the authority of the police, of having formed associations with a view to overthrow the existing order of society, of having declared against the existence of private property, and thereby inciting to a war of classes; they were accused, moreover, of teaching doctrines subversive of public morality, and incompatible with the existence of a well-ordered state. Upon a subsequent occasion Michel Chevalier, as the responsible editor of the 'Globe,' was included in the summons, and had to respond to similar charges; but the investigation of the case proceeded languidly, and it was not till the following August, and till they had given the Government still further provocation, that they were finally brought up for trial. In the meantime, however, they had to encounter a large amount of obloquy, and in fact some of the organs of the press were never tired of accusing them of swindling and inveigling youths into their communion without the consent of their parents; when pressed for evidence in support of these charges their accusers were never able to sustain them by proof, and, in default of a more convincing argument, one editor had recourse to a

hostile message. The Saint-Simonians refused to accept the challenge, on the ground that they were the
priests of a religion, and also because a thrust of the
sword could not establish the truth of the facts that
had been alleged. There were other journals, however, that behaved with much greater generosity.
None had been more bitter in its attacks, none had so
often used against them the terrible resources of ridicule as 'Figaro,' but it declares that it ceased to be
their enemy from the moment they became exposed to
the illegal proceedings of Government, and all the
sarcasm intended for them will fall upon a power that
has no energy except to persecute citizens, and to de-
prive them of their liberties. In a similar strain 'Le
Tribune,' though it disapproved of the doctrines of the
new sect, and contemplated an attack upon them, re-
frained at a time when it might appear to be the ally
of persecution.

The churches in the provinces were slowly recover-
ing from the shock they had received by the schism of
Bazard, and they now wrote to assure the church of
Paris of their entire sympathy and support. Letters
to that effect arrived from Metz, from Mulhouse, from
Strasbourg, from Lyons, Montpellier, Toulouse, Bordeaux, Nantes, Angers, Blois; from cities beyond the
Rhine and across the English Channel. They were
all filled with the same enthusiasm, and the same confidence. The interference of the law was a source of

M 2

rejoicing, not one of dismay; it hastened the decision
of the wavering, it redoubled the energy of the faithful. At Toulouse Rességuier was restored to his
former warmth. A Catholic priest was admitted into
the church, and Bruneau, a captain in the army, already
a convert, resigned his commission to devote himself
more exclusively to the cause. " I believed," said the
latter, " that the force of arms might be a powerful
means of emancipating the people. I was proud to
carry a sword, but now my mission is changed; I am
a Saint-Simonian, and I dedicate my whole life to the
work of an apostle. Now that our religion is exposed
to outrage and persecution, our Father has need of all
his children; honour summons me to his side. At a
period when there is no longer any political or religious belief—when doubt reigns in every mind, and
dissatisfaction in every breast,—it is well to show to the
world that there are men who feel they have a mission
to remedy these evils, and who have strength to devote
themselves to it."[44] While the church thus repaired
in the provinces the losses it had sustained in the capital, it also received assurances of sympathy from Germany. The ' Augsburg Gazette,' a paper having a
large circulation, published a letter ascribed to Henry
Heine, in which the doctrines of Saint-Simon were
very fairly expounded, and some admiration expressed
for the disciples. The writer describes the beneficial

[44] 'Œuvres,' vol. vi. p. 32.

1832.

effects produced by a system that had mitigated the
asperity entertained by the numerous disciples of Voltaire against the Christian faith, and had also in some
degree softened the violence of the revolutionary spirit. He concludes with exaggerated enthusiasm, that
if Saint-Simonism is an illusion, it is at least the most
sublime, the most profound, and the most powerful
illusion the world has ever seen.[65]

It was about this time that the last encounter took
place between M. Comte and the Saint-Simonians. M.
Michel Chevalier wrote an article, in which he alluded
to M. Comte as one of the disciples who had seceded
from the doctrines of Saint-Simon. Comte thought
it necessary to vindicate himself from the charge; he
confesses to having had very intimate relations with
Saint-Simon, which however ceased long before there
was any question of a sect, and before Saint-Simon
had adopted 'la couleur théologique.' The rupture,

[65] The year before, M. Carové had made the German public acquainted with the opinions of Saint-Simon, in his work, 'Der Saint-
Simonismus und die neuere französische philosophie' (Leipzig, 1831).
Three years afterwards, M. Moritz Veit published another learned exposition, 'Saint-Simon und der Saint-Simonismus' (Leipzig, 1834).
He says, "Es kommt hier, wie bei jeder Neuerung, nur darauf an sich
an die neue Anschauungsweise zu gewöhnen, um Erscheinungen wahr
zu nehmen die uns sehen entgangen sind. Und gerade dies ist ein
Hauptverdienst Saint-Simons, dass er das geistige Auge schärft und
eine Fülle neuer Ideen und Gesichtspunkte in uns anregt" (p. 108).
The year after, M. Parma wrote an essay, 'Del Sansimonismo,' (Milano,
1835,) in which he introduced the new ideas into Italy. So early as
1831 lectures upon the subject had been delivered at Paris in Italian.

1832. Comte adds, between them was in fact caused in some measure by the appearance in Saint-Simon of a "religious tendency profoundly incompatible with the philosophical direction which is my peculiar province." Comte admits that he had contributed articles to the 'Producteur' from November, 1825, to April, 1826; but the editors of that paper were quite unknown to him personally, and he was never present at any of their meetings; he ceased these contributions the moment he discovered the religious tendencies of the paper. His articles were nothing but developments of his 'Politique Positive,' which had been published in 1822; he is, therefore, surprised that he should be suspected of owing anything to the "Pères saint-simoniens." "It is, on the contrary, very certain that my conversation and writings have contributed to the political and philosophical education of your present chiefs, which certainly causes me no regret, except that they should not have better profited by them." But it is, he adds, astonishing that he should be confounded with men who, having been brought up under the Saint-Simonian fathers, have since then seen fit to separate from them,—"ce que je regarde d'ailleurs comme une grande preuve de bon sens." He contrasts his own method of laborious investigation with the easy elaboration of vague theories, in which the only condition of success is to let the imagination run riot. "Il est surtout très-attrayant, je l'avoue, pour ceux qui visent à la quantité des suffrages beaucoup plus qu'à leur qualité, après avoir adhéré à trois ou quatre épigraphes sacramentelles et sans prendre d'autre peine que celle de composer quelques verbeuses homélies, de se trouver tout-à-coup un grand homme, du moins momentanément, aux yeux d'un cercle assez nombreux, par lequel d'ailleurs on a l'avantage d'être vénéré comme un modèle de vertu. Ajoutez que la voie saint-simonienne conduit à la fortune et la mienne à la misère, et vous aurez achevé de démontrer que j'ai suivi une fort mauvaise direction. Cependant, Monsieur, je suis tellement obstiné que je ne voudrais pas en changer, quoique je sois assez jeune pour pouvoir le faire avantageusement. L'estime et la sympathie d'un très-petit nombre d'esprits éminents, juges compétents de mes travaux, telle est la seule grande récompense que se soit jamais proposée mon ambition, trop modeste ou trop élevée, comme vous croirez devoir l'entendre." The tone of Comte's letter was certainly far from conciliatory, and it is perhaps not surprising that Michel Chevalier, then a young man, should in his reply have been betrayed into undue warmth. He accuses Comte of ingratitude to a man to whom he owes everything : his lectures on the ' Philosophie Positive,' then in course of delivery, were but a development of the ' Politique Positive' of 1822, which was in its turn but an expansion of the ' Lettres de Genève.' It is to be regretted that Chevalier was not satisfied with this highly unjust statement; he even condescended to personalities. "Vous," he said, "qui n'aimez que vous-même, vous qui vivez toujours et partout en face de votre personalité. . . . Le bonheur vous a fui de plus en plus, vous avez vécu solitaire, inquiet, sans trouver un seul homme qui voulût s'attacher à vos pas. Il n'y a pas de joie pour l'homme isolé, il n'y a pour lui que fiel et amertume." Now, it happens that one of the very noblest traits in the generally unamiable character of Comte was this patient elaboration of his great work in the midst of the comparative solitude and poverty of his youth.[66]

Notwithstanding the large demands that had been made upon the liberality of the Saint-Simonians, the funds of the society were nearly exhausted. Indeed, at the time when they collected the most, their expenses were always larger than their resources. The 'Globe' newspaper was a serious charge, for the copies were for the most part distributed gratuitously. During the preceding summer the paper was often printed in the evening without any certainty that the morning would bring sufficient money to pay for the postage; at length, in April of this year it was finally discontinued. Its last numbers contained some able articles by M. Michel Chevalier, in which the sobriety of the future economist is enlivened by the enthusiasm of the

[66] Compare 'Œuvres,' vol. v. pp. 102–124; Littré, *op. cit.* pp. 189–201.

follower of Enfantin. Among other papers there was one upon what he chose to call the Mediterranean system; in it he proposed the construction of railways throughout Europe to an extent that then appeared wildly impracticable, but which has since been greatly surpassed in reality. The various lines were to concentrate towards the Mediterranean, and from thence, by improved navigation, communication with the East would be opened, to the great benefit of Europe; and the facilities that would be offered for travelling from one country to another would speedily break down the barriers of ancient prejudice, remove hereditary animosities, and finally cement nation to nation in a lasting peace. To this view of the influence of railways, which may not be wholly chimerical, he added a suggestion that unhappily has not yet been adopted; he proposed that the armies of Europe, instead of being applied to the destruction of property and life, should be employed upon works of public utility. He wrote at a period when the greatest misery existed among the labouring classes in France, and when a severe epidemic of cholera raged at Paris. The disciples spared no efforts to mitigate that terrible disease; those among them who were doctors offered their services gratuitously, and they petitioned that the Salle Taitbout, which had been closed by the police, might be reopened as a hospital. Michel Chevalier exhorted the Government

to employ the destitute upon public works, in order
to save them from starvation.   He pointed out the
improvements that were necessary in the streets of
Paris, many of which have since been executed by the
late Prefect of the Seine.   While the Saint-Simonians
were thus vindicating their sincerity by noble deeds
and earnest counsel, Enfantin declared that the first
part of his mission was already accomplished.   He had
summoned the oppressed portion of the human race
—women and the poor—to a new destiny; he had announced the approach of Universal Association, and
the abolition of Domesticity, the last trace of serfdom.   He had sufficiently spoken, it was now his duty
to act.   But, before he entered upon this new phase,
he would withdraw for a time from the world.   Both
he and his disciples were in need of rest; they were
exhausted by the labours they had undergone, but
especially were they oppressed by the calumnies that
had been heaped upon them, and the mockery that
had been directed against them.   Upon the day
that the 'Globe' ceased to appear, Enfantin retired
to Ménilmontant.[67]

[67] M. Louis Reybaud has been at some trouble to print a manuscript
"où sont déposées les idées écloses dans la retraite.   Toute la métaphysique du Saint-Simonisme, son Catéchisme et sa Genèse se trouvent
dans cet écrit, résumé de plusieurs conférences de la famille et inti-
tulé, 'Le Livre Nouveau.'"   I must refer the reader to the document
itself (see 'Socialistes Modernes,' vol. i. p. 126), which is to me quite
incomprehensible in the original, and the translation of portions of it,

III.

Ménilmontant is situated upon rising ground, within the fortifications of Paris; there Enfantin possessed a large house and garden, where his youth had been passed, and where at intervals in his busy and excited life he was wont to seek quiet and rest. Upon this occasion, however, he did not go alone; he brought with him forty of his most attached disciples, with whom he determined to share all the rigours of monasticism. His peculiar views of marriage had exposed him to the charge of licentiousness, for which, however, there was no exceptional foundation. He had always explained that his teaching was purely theoretical, and till the female Messiah had completed the emancipation of women it was impossible for him to regulate his conduct by any other than the established usages of society. He did not, however, pretend to practise mortifications, to which he attached no merit. He records with some satisfaction his fidelity for three years to a lady of tarnished reputation, whom he had accidentally encountered in the street. Subsequently he formed another fugitive attachment which resulted in the birth of a son, to whom he gave his name, and to whom he bequeathed a portion of his

with which Mr. Sargant has favoured us, is, if possible, more so (see 'Social Innovators'). It is satisfactory to find M. Reybaud confess that it sets forth " des choses que souvent, il faut l'avouer avec franchise, je ne comprenais pas moi-même."

fortune. But now he determined by a rigorous decree to remove every foundation for calumny; he decided that at Ménilmontant the severest asceticism should be observed,—the husband was to be separated from his wife, and the lover from his mistress. It is curious to read the letters of these ladies; some of them shared the enthusiasm of their husbands, and joyfully accepted with them their share in the sacrifice, but others were inclined to complain that a religion that had promised to consecrate happiness should so soon be induced to sanction the foulest assault fanaticism has ever made against it.[68] Enfantin, however, answered that the trial would be only for a time, So soon as the Messiah they looked for had come, a reign of love would recompense the mortified saints for the painful ordeal through which they were now to pass. Upon the day of their retreat Enfantin suffered a severe affliction in the death of his mother, after a few hours' illness from cholera. Such was the state of want to which he was

[68] Cécile Fournel writes to her husband—" On Wednesday I shall see you assume the dress of an apostle, and then I can give you but a sisterly kiss. I will endeavour to collect all my strength to hear you renounce me as wife, and your Amelia as child. Such a proceeding requires an energy which, I trust, I shall possess. Receive the tender farewell of her who will soon no longer be able to subscribe herself—your Cécile." She says to another correspondent, " I am sensible of the aim to which his noble and generous heart leads him when he separates himself from me. This knowledge is sufficient for me to accept the sacrifice, and, after all, what is my grief, what are my tears when the enfranchisement of the world is concerned?" (' Œuvres,' vol. vii. pp. 87, 88.)

reduced, that it was only through the generosity of his friends that he could pay her funeral expenses. With that love of ostentation that never forsook him, even in the hour of his severest trial, he determined that the ceremony should be imposing. He followed her remains to Père-la-Chaise, accompanied by all the disciples who were then at Paris; the procession numbered a thousand persons, among whom many were, no doubt, attracted by curiosity. From the cemetery he continued his way with the same parade to Ménilmontant, where, before the crowd separated, he enacted a dramatic scene. Standing before the people, he invited in a loud voice all who during the past year had lost a female relative, to come and receive his embrace; many obeyed, and the bereaved men fell sobbing into one another's arms; he then retired with his disciples into his own ground, and shut the door against the world.

Their first object was to produce what they somewhat fantastically called a "change of skin." [69] They were for the most part men who had been brought up in the Polytechnic School, and whose hands were unused to work, except with the pen. But it was a part of their creed that labour, even of the humblest de-

---

[69] "J'avais dit, un jour, que notre hiérarchie avait la peau trop blanche pour prétendre sauver le peuple; je l'ai noircie peu à peu : il m'a fallu à moi-même sept mois pour *changer de peau :* tous n'ont pas pu opérer cette transformation." ('Œuvres,' vol. ix. p. 19.)

scription, is a religious act, and they, therefore, undertook to perform for themselves all the functions of servants and labourers. Both the house and grounds had fallen into great disorder, and before they could be made a desirable habitation much was necessary to be done. The disciples executed everything themselves : civil engineers and doctors, professors of literature and professors of music, officers who had retired from the army, and gentlemen of independent fortune might be seen engaged upon the rudest work. Some were digging in the garden or plucking weeds from the path; others were painting the rooms or polishing the floor. They did not even shrink from the humblest domestic service; some were employed as housemaids, some as cooks, and others attended at table. Besides this the father had several disciples of inferior order in the hierarchy, to act as his personal attendants. In this manner did they seek to impart their own dignity to the humblest duties to which they were appointed; and having withdrawn for a time from the world, they endeavoured to form themselves into a family, without any of the ancient traditions of servility. These pursuits were generally enlivened by music, and when they were finished they were succeeded by others of a more intellectual order. Michel Chevalier and Lambert lectured on astronomy, geology, or physical geography; David instructed them in music; Fournel, who had returned to the fold, gave lessons in engineering. It must not be thought, however, that they enjoyed uncontrolled liberty; their position has been described as one of perfect equality, under the despotism of a single individual. Enfantin in fact exercised a power that has rarely been rivalled; he united the authority of priest to that of legislator; and the influence of his character for a time subdued even the faintest murmur of opposition. It is almost incredible, but yet can hardly be disputed, that his disciples regarded him with a superstitious awe; they seem to have accepted him as a messenger of heaven —a being endowed with exceptional attributes, and to whom it was necessary to yield implicit obedience. He declared that his life was a perpetual communion; yet he could not conceal from himself that he was not a divinity, for he occasionally experienced the suffering of mortals. "I wish, however," he said, "to be the father of mankind." [70] We have already seen the language which it was not thought inappropriate to address to him; and at Ménilmontant he was treated with a corresponding reverence. Every day an imposing ceremony took place at dinner: the father occupied an elevated position surrounded by ten chief apostles; in front of him, at a lower level, there extended to the end of the long room two parallel tables, at which sat the disciples of humbler rank in the hierarchy. The meal began and ended with music, and its solemnity

[70] 'Œuvres,' vol. vii. p. 75.

1832.   was of the nature of a religious rite. Upon certain
days of the week the public enjoyed the privilege of
viewing this highly dignified spectacle; and we are
informed that no one could escape the effect produced
by the attitude of the Father, such was the beauty of
his countenance, uniting at once the sublimity of
repose and the majesty of power. Nor were the disciples less objects of curiosity; at a period when
beards were never worn, they chose to defy the cus-
tom of society, and to let them grow to a prodigious
length. Their female admirers were as little pleased by
this manifestation of manhood, as by the voluntary re-
nunciation of its privileges through the adoption of a
celibate life. It was determined also still further to
mark the exceptional character of their mission, by the
adoption of a peculiar costume. A day was fixed, upon
which the change of dress was to be effected with a
ceremony becoming the importance of the event. There
happened to be a riot in Paris at the time on the occasion of the funeral of Lamarque, and the sound of
cannon, and even the voices of the combatants mingled
with the peaceful hymns and strange fantastic speeches
of the faithful at Ménilmontant. They had prepared
for the ceremony with becoming gravity, and indeed it
was a solemn occasion for them. Enfantin compares
his feelings to those of a priest at the hour of ordination, or of a cavalier who was about to receive the
religious order of knighthood. Were not they too

entering upon an apostleship in the sanctity of which   1832.
they believed as firmly? Were not they too submit-   June 6th.
ting to obligations as binding to redress the wrongs
they found in the world?   It may be that their extravagant conduct and still more extravagant language
were better suited to excite the ridicule than to inspire
the admiration of men, but that they were sincere
even in their wildest vagaries admits of little question;
and there never yet was enthusiasm unaccompanied by
extravagance. They were about to receive and admi-
nister vows that would bind them to encounter every
danger, to undergo every labour that might contribute
to relieve the poor from the burden of their poverty, and
to free woman from her subordination to man.   For
three days Enfantin withdrew from his disciples, that
he might prepare himself in solitude for the mission
that was before him. Even this short absence was
keenly felt by his admiring disciples. " Father," said
Talabot, " you are beloved by your children. They
are grieved by your absence; every time that your
name is pronounced at table a religious thrill steals
through the breasts of your children. Father, you
will be venerated upon your return into the midst of
us, and we will respect one another for your sake."
The happy moment at length arrived; at two o'clock
on Wednesday, June 6th, Enfantin returned to Ménilmontant. His disciples were drawn up in regular
order to meet him. He advanced with head un-

covered, preceded by two of the faithful, and followed
by five others; Michel Chevalier walked by his side.
As soon as the procession appeared, the family broke
forth into the chant—

"Hail! Father! Hail!
Hail! and glory to God!"

Enfantin entered the circle of his followers, and regarded them silently. "The children who had been
separated from him for three days leaped with joy; a
religious emotion became visible in every countenance,
and in the attitude of the whole assembly." Then Barrault rose and welcomed the Father's return to the
place of his birth, which he described as the Bethlehem
of the infant faith. He said that the disciples were
now ready to enter upon their new mission, and he
solemnly claimed the privilege of wearing the dress of
an apostle. They had finished their work of doc-
trinaires; they had sufficiently diffused their opinions
among the learned through the press; and now they
had gathered strength in the solitude of their retreat,
both by the exercise of manual labour and the rigid
practice of celibacy, to go forth with power as apostles
of the poor. Enfantin told them of the sacrifice he
had just accomplished, and invited them to imitate his
example. On that very morning he had renounced
the property he still possessed; he would no more
attach his name to any legal document; he would free

himself completely from the distractions of the world,
and he would separate himself from what the Christians call its pomps and vanities; he would gain each day, by the labour of his own hand, or head, his daily bread, in order to identify himself the more thoroughly with the poor to whom he was to preach. He then proceeded to lay aside his old apparel, and to clothe himself in the sacerdotal garments which he was to wear for the future; the moment his toilet was completed, an ensign was hoisted from the flag-staff upon the terrace to announce to the tumultuous· city below that the new era of peace had already dawned. Others of the disciples then followed his example, but some were faint-hearted and hesitated. M. Petit appealed to his mother for her consent, which she for the moment refused; yet Mme. Petit was one of the most ardent disciples, and her wealth was largely devoted to the necessities of the faith. Another confessed that he could not quench the fire of a terrestrial love that burned in his heart, but he trusted he might yet gain strength to do so. Raymond Bonheur, who had previously admitted his amatory proclivities with praiseworthy candour, trembled at the sacrifice required of him; he faltered for a little, but finally triumphed over his weakness. The costume is described as simple, and even becoming. "Justaucorps ·bleu à courtes basques, ceinture de cuir vernis, casquette rouge, pantalon de coutil blanc, mouchoir noué en sau-

toir autour du cou; cheveux tombant sur les épaules,
peignés et lissés avec soin; moustaches et barbes à
l'orientale." But the most remarkable feature was the
waistcoat, the pattern of which was perhaps supplied
by a neighbouring institution at Charenton. It was
intended to be symbolical of the dependence of one
man upon his fellow-men, and in order that the wearer
might be constantly reminded of this circumstance, it
was made in such a manner that no one could either
put it on or take it off, except with the assistance of a
valet. The breast was adorned with the name of the
disciple printed in large letters, and possessed the inconvenience that the wearer could not hope to escape
detection if the weakness of the flesh betrayed him into
a violation of his monastic vows. The ceremony of the
toilet was completed in the midst of a violent shower
of rain and the noise of cannon and thunder; yet this
did not prevent them from marching round the garden
in procession, before entering the house, singing, "Peuple, si notre voix réclame." In the following July they
commenced the erection of their first temple, in the
ground attached to their house. They were assisted
by labourers from Paris, chosen from among those who
were attached to the Saint-Simonian mission. Their
labours were enlivened by music and song, and by the
imposing spectacle of the Father, till they were agreeably interrupted by dinner on the lawn; they sat
down to the number of seventy-two, and commenced

operations with a Grace, which possessed at least the
rare merit of being sensible.

> " Dieu, par nos bras unis,
> Fertilise le monde,
> Nos travaux sont bénis.
> Dieu, par le fruit de la terre féconde
> Répare notre vigueur,
> Gloire à Dieu ; à vous, Père, merci ! "

The only drawback to their felicity was the immense
crowd that assembled to witness their proceedings ;
it is said that no less than 5000 persons passed
through the gate upon that day, and as many as 2000
were present at dinner. The proceedings were far-
ther enlivened by the arrival of the police, who had
orders to break up the reunion, and even the family.
The eloquence of Chevalier, however, averted this
catastrophe, and the officious visitors withdrew till a
more convenient season. In truth, the monks of Ménilmontant were now placed under very strict surveil-
lance : the paternal government resolved that the
people should not be corrupted by their dangerous
neighbours ; and taking advantage of the law against
illegal assemblies, soldiers were stationed under the
command of the police, at the entrance to the house, so
as to prevent the curious public from again joining in
the proceedings of the family. These were soon to be
of a very mournful character ; a disciple, M. Talabot,
was attacked with cholera, and died after a short illness ; the agony of his last moments was calmed by

1832.   music, executed on the piano in an adjacent room, by David. So favourable an opportunity for display could not of course be lost : the body was laid on a bed of state, at the foot were placed the sacred garments of. the apostleship, and the police regulations having been relaxed, vast crowds passed through the room to view the remains of the dead. The funeral was conducted with appropriate solemnity ; the *cortége* was preceded by police, and followed by large numbers of disciples arrayed in their new costume, and by others whom curiosity had attracted. The grave at Père-la-Chaise was dug by the Saint-Simonians themselves,—an act which was, we are told, symbolical of the new dignity which has been imparted to every form of labour. Barrault approached the coffin and addressed the crowd that had collected. " Behold," he said, " the Apostles before you—one lying there, the others standing around, but all alike living in the bosom of God."[71] Of those who took part in this mournful ceremony, all were not mere idle dreamers ; it is recorded that many civil engineers of eminence and wealthy capitalists were present ; and that from the acquaintance that sprang up among them upon that occasion, the railway from Paris to Saint-Germain is due. It required indeed three years of incessant agitation before the Government would make the necessary concession ; but this work was actively carried on by Péreire in

[71] ' Œuvres, vol. vii. pp. 172, 175.

the 'National,' Flachat in the 'Constitutionnel,' and M. Chevalier in the 'Débats.' These names are all intimately connected with Saint-Simonism, and it was to M. Péreire himself that the concession was finally granted. The funeral of Talabot was speedily followed by the death of Bazard. Enfantin at once sought to display his magnanimity. For some time past Bazard could not conceal the disgust with which the extravagance of Enfantin inspired him. " Enough," he said, " of these costumes on lay-figures, of these words without meaning, of these movements without result. The entire school is degenerating into the puerile and the fantastic." He describes his own position with some bitterness : while the disciples of Enfantin are accustomed to see revelations and worlds daily emanating from the fervent brains of D'Eichthal or Duveyrier, he has been languishing with disease. Without money, without followers, there has been no one to keep the public informed as to " the divine calm of his face," or the " smiling majesty of his countenance." Yet without these advantages he has maintained a correspondence which when published will, he says, form the true continuation of his master's work ; and the few extracts we possess are not without merit. In one of these he complains that, to his great regret, it has been repeatedly said among the Saint-Simonians that " from the present day we enter upon a new era when there will be no more pain nor sacrifice ; when

1832. death will be a joy and divorce a *fête*; when the improvement and preservation of society will neither require privation nor abnegation on the part of any of its members. It is possible to justify this illusion; but it will not the less continue an illusion. Certainly man ought not to bow passively under misery, and accept it with resignation as a necessity from which there is no escape; he ought, on the contrary, to oppose it actively with the faith which he derives from the power he possesses to deliver himself from its empire. Neither ought he to consider this sacrifice as an eternal law; trusting, on the contrary, in infinite goodness, he should see in it nothing but a transient evil, and labour to lessen it, till finally it disappears. But so long as humanity has not attained this term of its development, so long as a disproportion continues between its desires and its capabilities to satisfy them, so long as perfect harmony does not exist between man and nature, between man and man,—so long misery, in different degrees, will be found amongst us; and in different degrees also during that time sacrifice will be a necessary condition of progress, and therefore a virtue."[72] Enfantin had always found in Bazard a formidable opponent, but now he sought to do honour to one who had been so long his colleague. Accordingly he collected his disciples together, arrayed in all the magnificence of their sacerdotal garments, and

[72] 'Œuvres,' vol. vii. p. 47.

proceeded to join the funeral *cortége*.   Bazard had
died at Courtry, some distance from Ménilmontant;
it was therefore necessary for the Saint-Simonians to
pass through several villages.   The reception they met
from the crowd collected by so unusual a spectacle was
generally courteous; upon one occasion only some dis-
paraging words were directed against them.   " The
calm and majestic figure of the Father," we are told,
" attracted the attention of all, and subdued the malice
of the scoffer."   As they proceeded they distributed
quantities of tracts along their line of march.   At last,
however, they were encountered by an agitated officer
of police who barred their passage, and required their
leaders to appear before the *maire* of Livry; that
bewildered functionary, after some consideration, permitted them to proceed.   But scarcely had they sur-
mounted one difficulty before they were met by another:
Jules Lechevalier appeared, bearing a message from
Mme. Bazard, to request Enfantin and his disciples to
return.   Mme. Bazard did not wish, he said, that the
man whom her husband regarded as having impaired
his mission, should visit his corpse while it was scarcely
cold.   Undismayed by this rebuke, Enfantin determined to proceed.   After a short time however, Jules
Lechevalier brought in a second message even more
explicit than the first, and then Enfantin unwillingly
yielded.   " I wish," he said, " to give this one addi-
tional proof of the respect I entertain for the liberty

1832.   of woman;" so saying, he ordered the retreat, and his mortified disciples returned at midnight to Ménil-montant.

The result of the examination before the police court in January had not been satisfactory, and the trial of the Saint-Simonians now impended. Enfantin, Chevalier, Barrault, Duveyrier, and Rodrigue, were commanded to appear at the Palais de Justice, at Paris, on the 27th August, charged with having held illegal meetings, and with having outraged public morality. In the interval, Michel Chevalier had taken care to make inquiries into the personal character of each of the judges; he communicated to Enfantin the information he obtained, and it was thought that it would enable the accused to reply with crushing force to any allegations of immorality that might be made against them. On the morning of the trial they left Ménilmontant with great ostentation; they were dressed in full costume, and accompanied by large numbers of the disciples. Amongst these were two ladies, Aglaé Saint-Hilaire, cousin to Enfantin, and Cécile Fournel. In the midst of the procession marched their leader, dressed in clothes of a lighter shade than the others, and upon his breast the words " Le Père." A large crowd were collected by this curious spectacle, but no hostile demonstration occurred. Upon entering the court, Enfantin with great self-possession seated himself in an arm-chair near the President, from which however, he was speedily ejected. The Saint-Simonians, relying upon the justice of their cause and upon their own ability, disdained to employ a regular advocate; they pointed to the two ladies, Madame Fournel and Mlle. Saint-Hilaire, as the only councillors they required. But the judge was inexorable upon this point; it was not permitted he said, for women to plead at the bar, and after an angry scene they were forced to retire. When the first witness for the defence was required, according to the usual form, to swear to speak without hatred or fear, and to tell the whole truth and nothing but the truth, he appealed for permission to Enfantin. This proceeding excited the indignation of the judge, who would not permit the witness to take an oath unless it was his own free act. Witness after witness was summoned, but they each followed the same course, and with the same result; at length the remainder were called for *en masse*, and were sent back after the others. M. Lambert explained the cause of this remarkable obstinacy. "The Attorney-General," he said, "has observed that when an oath is taken, it is taken before God. But as regards ourselves, while we acknowledge the Divinity, we acknowledge also among men, one who above all others is the interpreter of the will of God. You say that a witness has no need to ask the authorization of any man in such a matter, but you know not who this man is; this man is the most exalted manifestation of God in humanity. That is to say, we acknowledge the existence of a human power whose acts have a religious inspiration and sanction."[73]   M. Ollivier, when called upon, replied, "I am in the presence of my father, my judge, my director, and my guide; and my conscience will not permit me to take this oath without his permission."   At length the most eloquent apostles stood up and entered upon their defence. MM. Chevalier, Lambert, Duveyrier, and Barrault each spoke at great length, and wearied the patience of the court with a detailed explanation of their opinions.   Duveyrier was interrupted by the President on account of the violence of his language; he was told that if he could not moderate his tone an advocate must be named for him.   "An advocate!" he exclaimed, pointing to the bar; "where could one be found?   When I entered the court I told all that I was accused of having written that the world lives in prostitution and adultery; but this is true of all of you. Have courage then to acknowledge it, that is the only defence you can set up for us.   They would not do so, and therefore cannot defend us: they did not deny the charge; they looked down and answered not."[74]   Twenty years afterwards, a magistrate who had taken part in the trial confessed, that neither from the tribune nor the bar had he ever heard speeches that produced upon him so great an impression as those of Duveyrier.   But the most remarkable scene was reserved for the second

[73] 'Œuvres,' vol. vii. p. 224.   [74] Ib. p. 238.

day, for it was then that Enfantin spoke. He rose from his place with great gravity, and placing his right hand upon his breast he silently regarded the audience, the judge, and the jury. The judge fancied that the singular man before him was endeavouring to collect his thoughts and to recover from the nervousness to which inexperienced orators are so painfully liable; but Enfantin explained that his silence was produced by a very different cause. It was necessary he said, for him to regard his audience attentively, and also for them to regard him; only in that way could they come under the influence exercised by his appearance. His thoughts were best revealed in his countenance. The Attorney-General had yet to learn the full power of beauty; and in order that this lesson might be the more effectual, Enfantin paused from time to time in the course of his speech, and deliberately and silently regarded the court. Its impatience continued to increase, till at length it became quite uncontrollable. The Father, who had never for a moment withdrawn his eyes from the judges, continued to look at them silently and with an irritating calm. After a few minutes' consultation, the President rose angrily and said, "The hearing is suspended. We are not here to wait the result of your contemplations." Enfantin looked after the retreating functionaries, and then turned round smiling to the audience. "Behold," he said, "another proof of their incompetence!" The tenor of his speech

was as remarkable as his manner; he announced that
he had not come there to defend himself, he had come
to teach them. "I judge," he said, "but I cannot be
judged." The court was not of the same opinion,
and he and M. Chevalier were sentenced to a year's
imprisonment, and to pay 100 francs fine; Barrault
and Rodrigue escaped with a nominal fine of 50 francs
each. Several months however elapsed, before the
sentence was put into execution; it was not till the
December following, that Enfantin and Chevalier were
shut up at Sainte-Pélagie. In the interval, the life at
Ménilmontant was resumed, but its severity was relaxed. The government had been purely theocratical,
and the ascendancy of the Father over his disciples had
become so irresistible, that individual liberty appeared
to be completely effaced. It was necessary to modify
a state of things quite unsuited to the democratic tendencies of the time. Duveyrier, D'Eichthal, and Lambert were selected to exercise over the rest an authority, based entirely upon the moral influence of their
characters. The disciples were permitted to mix more
freely with the public, and only dined together twice
a week; at other times they frequented restaurants,
where they met men of the working classes, and while
enjoying a dinner at 15 sous, they had the opportunity
of propagating their opinions. But the greatest trial to
their fortitude was the obligation of celibacy. Their
enthusiasm and their faith in Enfantin had induced

them to resign lucrative employments, to bestow all
their property upon the infant church, to devote their
lives to its service, for its sake to encounter ridicule
and even persecution; [75] but the last burden that was
put upon them was too heavy even for their well-tried
faith; they accepted it indeed for a time, but it speedily
chilled their enthusiasm.   The husband pined for
his home, and the lover sighed once more for the smile
of his mistress; one by one they violated their pledges,
and deserted their "Father." The defection began
with Ribes, and the three disciples who were specially
charged with the supervision of morality found the current impossible to stem, and were themselves among
the first to yield to its force.   D'Eichthal predicted
that if ever the female Messiah should come, she would
find Enfantin alone. "Do not hope," he said, "to
preserve about you the groups of men by whom you
are surrounded now; the power of woman will remove them from you, and you will remain alone with
Holstein, and perhaps with Rigaud." The same day
he and Duveyrier left Ménilmontant, and threw aside
their grotesque costume; shortly afterwards many of
the principal members followed them.

[75] Michel Chevalier says, " Tous ou presque tous nous avons quitté,
pour le suivre, soit des professions honorables, soit une fortune honnête,
soit des positions qu'entoure la considération publique. Le fait peut
s'expliquer de deux manières : ou nous sommes tous devenus fous, ou
il est un homme prodigieux.   Pourquoi choisir de prime abord la
première hypothèse ? Pourquoi ne pas prendre la peine de vérifier la
seconde ? " (' Œuvres,' vol. viii. p. 26.)

D'Eichthal was received with open arms by his family; "Continue to dream if you please," said his father to him, "but do not separate yourself again from me." He had not however abandoned his Saint-Simonian faith, or his belief in Enfantin, and he preserved his beard carefully as a valuable memento of his life at Ménilmontant.

In the meantime, the finances of the Saint-Simonians did not improve; they had always been recklessly mismanaged. At one time no less than 5000 fr. were spent per month, and yet during this period of prosperity it frequently happened that not so much as a franc remained in their coffers,—their conduct was uniformly extravagant. When they retired to Ménilmontant and were obliged to suspend their lectures, they offered the use of their halls gratuitously, for musical and scientific purposes. They were now reduced to such straits, that for six months past they had been unable to pay the rent of their house in the Rue Monsigny, and the proprietor threatened to indemnify himself by seizing the property they had left behind. To add to their misfortunes, Enfantin and his former associate Rodrigue had to appear once more before the tribunal, to answer to a charge of swindling. They were however at once acquitted, and notwithstanding their embarrassment, they celebrated the result of the trial by a public dinner at the "Veau qui Tette." Amid these signs of dissolution, a part at least of the old vitality remained; a few

young men, of ardent dispositions, could not yet resist the fascination of Enfantin, and continued, from
time to time, to join the ranks of his disciples. Among
these, the most conspicuous was Eugène Hermann; he
was a son of the Minister of Finance, and from the prominent position occupied by his father, as well as his
own unhappy fate, the case attracted much attention.
More than a year before the time at which we have
arrived, he became a convert to Saint-Simonism. His
father, who acted throughout with greater harshness
than affection, sent him away from Paris to reside at
Strasbourg, with a clergyman of strictly orthodox views.
After a time he was permitted to proceed to Italy, and
to remain there for a year; but his banishment intensified rather than diminished his enthusiasm.

The persecution to which the Saint-Simonians had
been recently exposed still further excited in his
generous nature the desire to share their misfortunes;
this desire became at length irresistible. He travelled
from Naples to Paris without stopping by the way, he
presented himself to Enfantin and begged to be admitted into the family. As soon as the ceremony of
initiation was completed, and he had assumed the robes
of the Apostleship, he communicated with his father.
The indignation of the minister was so great that he refused to see his son. The unhappy youth, exhausted
by the fatigue of his rapid journey, and the excitement
by which it was followed, could not obtain rest either

o

night or day. In this condition the severity of his
father's conduct shook his reason; he became deliri-
ous, and had to be removed from Ménilmontant to the
asylum of Esquirol.

It was a favourite opinion of Enfantin that the
press and the theatre are the two principal means
of teaching the people; the first might be made
to correspond to theology, or the exposition of
dogma, the latter to religious worship. Through
the 'Globe' he had availed himself of the one, and
he now sought by pompous ceremonies and *fêtes*,
by music and fantastic costumes, to rival the po-
pularity of the other. "When we shall have," he
said, "three hundred men, properly robed, mingled
with women, carrying symbols, and when they shall
have been taught to sing as the choirs of Greece, fore-
telling the future of the people, of woman, and of art,
—not a single soul will remain unmoved, all will be
ready to ejaculate Amen." But while he endeavoured
to organize imposing spectacles at Ménilmontant,
he did not forget the provinces. In truth many of the
disciples who still remained faithful to their master
began to suffer from the monotonous and even rude
life at Ménilmontant. Fournel was already released
from his celibate vows, and having rejoined his wife
he resumed the active work of an apostle. Barrault
so early as June had advised the family to disperse to
the four quarters of the globe, and to carry with them

the message of peace. " Then," he said, " that familiarity which exists at present will terminate ; Enfantin will become really a king, and the deceitful parody of royalty which surrounds him now will disappear."[76] It was not, however, till October that his advice was adopted. The monastic life they had led was not without its advantages. It had made, we are told, energetic characters ; it had distinguished the men of the new era from those of the old, it had familiarized them with rough work, which had produced its desirable result in a " change of skin ;" and above all, the strictness of the discipline that had been submitted to was a conclusive answer to the malevolent charges that had been made against them. At length Hoart and Bruneau left on a mission to Lyons, and shortly afterwards they were followed by others. The occasion of their departure was of course celebrated with due formality : Enfantin and the remnant of his followers accompanied them a part of the way ; they visited the various stations memorable in the annals of the faith—the spot where Enfantin had taken part in the defence of Paris, and the house where, acting the part of midwife, he had ushered his illegitimate child into the world. Their progress was interrupted by many fine speeches and some sacred music, and then, having received the blessings of the Father and the apostles, they continued their route. Enfantin and Michel Chevalier

[76] ' Œuvres,' vol. vii. p. 129.

1833. returned to Ménilmontant, where they remained till
the 15th of December, when the doors of the prison of
Sainte-Pélagie were closed upon them. From that
moment Enfantin released his disciples from his
authority; he still recommended the practice of
celibacy and the adoption of the peculiar costume,
but every one was free to take the measures that
seemed to him best for the propagation of the faith.
Yet certain general instructions emanated from time to
time from the imprisoned apostles.[77]

The missionaries were desired to exact a profession
of faith from their converts, which was conceived in
these terms :—

" I believe in God, the father and mother of all, who
is eternally good.

" I believe in God, who is infinite in love, wisdom,
science, beauty, and strength.

" I believe that God has raised up Saint-Simon to
teach the Father through Rodrigue.

" I believe that God has raised up the Father to summon the Female Messiah, who will consecrate a union
of perfect equality between man and woman, between
humanity and the world.

" [77] Mais ce qu'Enfantin ne pouvait ni abdiquer ni perdre, c'était sa
supériorité morale et intellectuelle, c'était l'amour, le respect et l'influence que cette supériorité devait lui faire obtenir partout et toujours ;
c'était le désir ardent, la passion profondément religieuse dont il était
plus que jamais embrasé, de mettre toutes ses facultés, tout son être,
au service de DIEU PÈRE et MÈRE et de l'HUMANITÉ *homme* et *femme*."
— *Œuvres*, vol. ix. p. 3.

"Friends of the Father, this is my faith. I beg to 1833. be admitted among your brethren, in order that I may devote my life, like you, to prepare the triumph of the Father and the advent of the Mother, by in-creasing the comfort, the happiness, and the hopes of the people.

> "Love to God.
> Glory to the Father.
> Hope for the Mother."

And after this confession a collar was placed round his neck, each bead representing a distinguished Saint-Simonian disciple. The missions were continued with unabated vigour during the imprisonment of Enfantin, and occasionally the apostles encountered violent op-position from the fanaticism of the people. Terson preached among the mountains of Roussillon and the Pyrenees; at times he was forced to live on the herbs and roots he gathered by the way, at others he joined in the coarsest work, and taught his fellow-workmen the simple songs of the faith, in which they were encouraged to look forward to a time when the burden of their labour would be lightened. As he approached a town, not far from Perpignan, he was met by forty youths, who invited him to tarry amongst them and to cheer them with his words of hope. The mayor per-mitted him to preach from a balcony in the market-place to upwards of 2000 persons, who frequently in-terrupted him with their applause. At Perpignan itself his reception was not so favourable : mounted gen-

1833.   darmes arrested him and brought him before the *préfet*,
but when his papers were examined they were found
to be satisfactory, and he was set at liberty. He was
visited by the notable personages in the town, and entertained at a banquet in the evening. On the following morning, however, he was again arrested, and kept
for five days in prison; he was then released, but he
was conducted by gendarmes to the frontier of the department.   He, however, continued to preach the
gospel, traversing Narbonne, Béziers, Montpellier,
Nîmes, Tarascon, and Marseilles. At the same time
other missionaries, not less zealous, were scattered
throughout Burgundy and the Jura. Wherever they
went they met with manifestations of sympathy, which
more than compensated them for the sarcasm and the
insults they occasionally had to endure. They even
penetrated so far as Baden and Würtemberg and
Bavaria, but there they were not well received, and
were forced to retire. Similion became acquainted
with Saint-Simonism in Paris, and was intoxicated by
its noble views of perfectibility; he returned to his
native country of Savoy, and at Chambéry he collected
around him a few friends, to whom he communicated
his enthusiasm. Although compelled by poverty to
cultivate the ground, he yet found time to propagate
the faith; he attracted crowds of peasants on Sun-
days, and preached to them in the mountain villages.
At length the clergy took offence and denounced him

1833.

from their pulpits; the bishop presided over a meeting, at which his destruction was resolved upon. In vain his friends supplicated him to fly for safety, he was deaf to their appeal; he determined to await the persecution, and to endure the suffering as became a worthy apostle. Upon Christmas Day the *curé* of his parish required him to attend Mass; he refused. Two days afterwards he was arrested, his books and correspondence were seized, he was handcuffed in the presence of his terrified mother, and led away to the prison at Moutiers. Two months elapsed without trial, and then he was visited by a local authority, who promised him his liberty if he would sign a recantation. Nothing would induce him to do so, and numbers of sympathizing friends visited him in his cell, to the great displeasure of his persecutors, who had him removed in consequence to the prison of Fénestrelle. For two months longer he languished in a damp and miserable dungeon, in company with other prisoners, who were much worse off than himself, for they were not supported by his faith; to them he explained how in a short time all prisons would be abolished and converted into national workshops. He was at length brought to trial, and sentenced to pass four months longer in prison and to cease to preach his dangerous doctrines.

Nor was Similion the only missionary whose zeal was reproved by the law; another, named Vidal, issued

1833.   a religious manifesto to the people at Montpellier, for
which he was thrown into prison. After the expiration
of five months he was at length brought to trial, and
acquitted. If these cases have been correctly reported,
they are unquestionably disgraceful to the administration of justice in France.

Enfantin devoted the weary months of his imprisonment to the arrangement of the papers belonging to
the faith, and their careful annotation ; he also composed a new calendar, in which the days of the month
and week were called after the distinguished apostles
of Saint-Simonism.   During the same period two
newspapers were started, ' La Tribune des Femmes '
and ' Le Livre des Actes.'   They were edited by
ladies, Madame Cécile Fournel and Madame Suzanne,
and were devoted to advocating the doctrines of Saint-
Simonism and recording the progress of conversion.
The monotony of the life at Sainte-Pélagie was
agreeably diversified by a new trial. Enfantin and
Chevalier were brought before the court in April, to
reply to the charge of having continued at Ménilmontant to hold illegal meetings. The Father took care
to appear in an imposing costume : upon his shoul-
ders he wore a velvet mantle ornamented with ermine,
round his neck was the collar with the mystic beads,
a scarf fell gracefully over his chest, upon it his long
beard rested, and beneath was seen the symbolical
waistcoat, buttoned from behind ; this toilet was com-

pleted by immense boots that came up to his knees. Never were his words more powerful; he explained, that as Christ was the son of man who came to reveal God the Father to the world, he, Enfantin, was the son of man and woman, who was commissioned to reveal both God the father and God the mother. Michel Chevalier, who was included in the indictment, did not follow the extravagance of his master; the day before the trial he shaved his beard, and he appeared in the court in the ordinary dress of humanity. Both the accused were acquitted. Shortly afterwards Chevalier, at the instance of Enfantin, made efforts to regain his liberty; in this he was successful. The term of his imprisonment was shortened, and his future success was not impaired by the follies of his youth. When he left prison he was but twenty-seven years of age; after a short time spent in America, he returned to France and commenced a prosperous career on the staff of the 'Journal des Débats;' he subsequently rose to the highest honours in the empire. On the 1st of August, Enfantin likewise obtained the pardon of the king, and left Sainte-Pélagie; he hastened to rejoin his father. We are told that when he pressed to his heart the author of his noble life, every eye moistened with tears to behold the inspired of God, the man who is animated by a boundless love, caress his old father with such touching simplicity.

IV.

While Enfantin was still languishing in prison, Barrault undertook a mission to the east. He had long contemplated this enterprise, and he at length received the authorization of his master. " You may," said Enfantin, " announce ME to the east, and summon the Mother."[78] In the early days of April, 1833, he embarked at Marseilles, on board ' La Clorinde' for Constantinople; he was accompanied by thirteen disciples, all dressed in their apostolic costume. It chanced that Garibaldi was one of the passengers, and he has recorded in his ' Mémoires' the impression the Saint-Simonians made upon him. " The apostle," he says, " proved to him that the man who defends his own country, or who attacks another, is but a soldier —pious in the one case, unjust in the other; but that the man who makes himself a cosmopolitan, and who offers his sword and his blood to every nation struggling against tyranny, is more than a soldier—he is a hero. Then a strange light broke in upon my mind, which enabled me to see that a ship is more than a mere means of transport, it became a winged messenger bearing the word of the Lord and the sword of the archangel. I had started eager for adventure, curious for new scenes, and wondering whether that irresistible vocation which I had believed was to be

[78] ' Œuvres,' vol. viii. p. 212.

simply that of a captain ' au long cours ' had not
for me another horizon, yet unperceived. I caught
a glimpse of that horizon through the mist that
covers the future." On the 15th of April, ' La
Clorinde' anchored at Constantinople. As soon as
the disciples touched land, they " rendered homage,"
speaking out loud, and with their hats off, to the
daughters of the East, poor and rich, on foot or in
carriages. Their strange gestures and curious costume caused no small astonishment. The Greeks
were at that time celebrating Easter, and large numbers had collected at Constantinople for the purpose;
the arrival of the Saint-Simonians was highly distasteful to them, and they evinced some signs of opposition.
Nor was the Turkish government likely to display
much zeal in defence of men who upheld doctrines
so little to their taste, concerning the emancipation of
women. Moreover, the conduct of the disciples was
such as to excite jealousy and alarm ; it appears that
every woman they happened to meet in the street
they made a point of saluting. This unusual proceeding greatly aggravated their unpopularity. They
were arrested, put on board a ship, treated with much
harshness, and conducted to Smyrna; they were
there received more favourably, and after the experience gained at Constantinople, they determined to act
in a less offensive manner. Barrault established a
centre of the faith at Smyrna, and then left for Alex-

1833.   àndria. "The Turkish race has heard the annuncia-
tion, it must now resound in the ears of the Arabs."[79]
When he arrived at Alexandria, he dispatched missionaries to Cairo, to the pyramids, to Damietta and
Rosetta. He then returned to Smyrna, stopping at
Rhodes, and from thence he sent apostles to Tenedos,
to Mitylene, to Scio, and to Candia. " Père," writes
Barrault, " ma tâche de prophète est accomplie : Stam-
boul, Smyrne et Alexandrie m'ont entendu. J'atten-
drai en silence la venue de la FEMME, pour qui seulement ma bouche s'ouvrira encore, en jetant un premier cri d'amour et d'enthousiasme."[80] While the
disciples were thus spreading the new gospel among
the islands of the archipelago and in the bazaars of the
East, Enfantin was released from his Western prison,
and he announced his intention of joining in the work.
But before he set out he declared that his policy had
changed ; enough, he said, had been done to diffuse a
knowledge of the doctrines of the new religion. The
rehabilitation of the flesh, the religious dignity of labour,
the equality of woman with man, the expected advent of
a female Messiah,—these views have been advocated
from the press and upon the platform, till all Europe has
resounded with them ; the appeal to women has even
assumed too great prominence, and it requires to be
moderated. It is necessary to remember that labour

[80] ' Œuvres,' vol. ix. p. 81.
[79] ' Œuvres,' vol. ix. p. 79.

is the real basis of the worship which God demands, and therefore industry and politics should recover their position, and even predominate for the future; "because," he says, "two whole years of our lives have been already devoted to only one aspect of our religion, and that is too much for apostles."[81] At present, a vast enterprise awaits initiation, to which the religious enthusiasm of the disciples may be fitly applied. This is no other than the construction of a canal to unite the Mediterranean with the Red Sea, a project so long entertained but not yet attempted. Everything points to the Saint-Simonians as the best adapted for the work. Their ranks are recruited from the Polytechnic School, and many of the disciples are civil engineers, while others are skilled mechanics, but all are animated by the strongest enthusiasm. Alone, of any class of men in Europe, they are willing to be the soldiers of a peaceful army, where glory will be the only reward for labour and privation.[82] These plans were matured at Sainte-Pélagie, and so soon as Enfantin regained his liberty, he issued a peremptory requisition to his disciples to supply him, by subscrip-

[81] 'Œuvres,' vol. ix. p. 60.

[82] Enfantin writes, "La percée de Suez, projetée depuis si longtemps, languit. Il faut qu'elle se fasse : elle se fera pour nous, ou à cause de nous. J'ai déjà vingt hommes en Égypte qui préparent. J'emmène avec moi cinq hommes encore. Plusieurs sont ingénieurs, et j'espère avant six mois pouvoir appeler à l'œuvre. Il faut que cette grande œuvre soit œuvre d'enthousiasme, comme l'était la guerre, et que la gloire paye ces soldats pacifiques."—Œuvres, vol. ix. p. 84.

tion, with money to enable him to carry them into execution.[83] His appeal was so far responded to that on the 23rd of September he embarked at Marseilles for Alexandria. He was accompanied by five of his disciples—Lambert, Holstein, Alexis Petit, Ollivier and Fournel, who once more abandoned his wife in the interests of the faith; during his absence, she remained at Paris, and occupied herself as editor of the 'Livre des Actes.' Before their departure they laid aside their peculiar costume, and shaved their beards. A like privilege was accorded to those who remained behind; they speedily availed themselves of it, and it was announced that there only remained seven persons in France who continued to wear the apostolic garments. " The frail bark," which, we are told, was " to carry the destinies of the world," was called the 'Prince héréditaire;' she was to sail early in the morning, and Enfantin with his disciples embarked the previous evening. During the whole night they continued on deck, surrounded by many friends, who had come to bid farewell; the anguish of parting was mitigated by music, and the songs of the faithful resounded in the darkness across the harbour. When day broke, the vessel weighed anchor, and those who remained behind solemnly intoned 'L'Appel,' till their straining eyes could no

[83] " Il me faut de l'argent," he writes; " cette fois je le demande, moi le Père, positivement, et personnellement, je le demande au nom de Dieu ; il le faut, l'œuvre est là."—*Œuvres*, vol. ix. p. 62.

longer discern 'Le Prince héréditaire.' The voyage was a tedious one, it was prolonged by contrary winds and calms to rather over a month; but, as we are informed God guided the ship, no harm could of course happen to it. At length it entered the port of Alexandria, flying the Saint-Simonian ensign, and the disciples who had gone before knew that the Father had arrived. Enfantin was cordially welcomed by M. Ferdinand de Lesseps, who was then the vice-consul, and he became for two months the guest of Soliman Bey, at Cairo; Fournel, in his capacity of civil engineer, readily gained access to the celebrated viceroy Mehemet Ali, and continued for upwards of five months to urge upon him the immense advantages that would result if a canal were to be cut to Suez, but although he was listened to patiently, his efforts were unsuccessful. In truth, Mehemet Ali was already bent upon another project, which appeared to be less chimerical, and, if successful, would be of more direct advantage to Egypt. This was the damming up of the Nile for purposes of irrigation; M. Linant and other French engineers had submitted plans for the execution of this design, and the Egyptian government, after some discussion, determined to adopt them. Fournel returned to France, and soon obtained employment upon the Paris and St. Germain railway, which was then in process of construction; but Enfantin, and many of his disciples, resolved to remain in Egypt, where, if they could not carry out the project they had formed, they could at least obtain other useful employment. Some had already applied their talents in various directions. David, who was afterwards to acquire European fame by his operas 'Herculanum' and 'Désert,' charmed the Alexandrians with concerts, where many of his own compositions were for the first time heard in public. Barrault drew an eager audience to his lectures, which were received with acclamations, and the 'Moniteur Egyptien' declared that "Alexandria, since the best days of its glory, has never heard within its walls a voice so eloquent, or a poetry of language so harmonious."[84] Lambert, on the other hand, was commissioned by the government to found a Polytechnic School at Cairo. Bruneau was appointed director of the school of artillery at Thora. Urbain and Granal were appointed professors at the school at Kanka. Alric, a sculptor, made a bust of the Pasha. D'Eichthal obtained employment from the Greek government. Fourcade and other medical men gave their services to the hospital. But the largest number of the disciples, under the leadership of Enfantin, determined to join in the works of the Nile, which were already begun by Linant. Enfantin and Linant were early brought into intimate relation through a common friend, M. Talabot, who had been very dear to both.

[84] 'Œuvres,' vol. ix. p. 179.

For a time everything prospered. Enfantin occu- 1834.
pied a tent near the works, and sought to attract by
his name other volunteers from France. He saw a
favourite idea of his master, Saint-Simon, on the point
of being realized, for the organization of a pacific army
of industry had been actually begun. "Linant has
requested to be authorized to form a corps of 12,000
regular labourers, disciplined, clothed, and lodged like
the regiments of the line, but under the command of
engineers, and embracing all the various handicrafts
required for constructions, preceded by a musical
band; the men should carry a pickaxe upon their
shoulder instead of a musket, and by their side a sur-
veyor's compass." Thus equipped, they might march
to a nobler warfare than any their forefathers
waged. The entire family of man might be united
under a single banner, and go forth to the conquest of
nature for their common benefit. The suggestion of
Linant was well received by the Government, and
there were only a few details wanting to render the
army complete; these were, however, never supplied,
and the scheme remained unachieved. Yet the construction of a dam in the regular manner continued for
a time with unabated vigour, and a large number of
labourers were employed upon it. It was during this
period that the Duke de Raguse visited Egypt, and has
left us a record of the impression the Saint-Simonians
made upon him. "I found," he says, "some of tho

1834. most celebrated apostles of that sect established in the
house of Soliman Pasha. He had received them well,
—indeed, he had proved a real Providence to them,
for they lived with him, and in the enjoyment of his
intimacy. Among others were the Father Enfantin,
the supreme head, MM. Barrault, Lambert, and Petit.
They all appeared to me to have agreeable manners, a
tolerant and compassionate character, and many soci-
able qualities ; among them were men of enlarged and
profound knowledge. Many came from the Polytechnic School. M. Lambert was a civil engineer in
France, and is a very distinguished man. M. Barrault is endowed with a natural eloquence, both brilliant and fascinating ; he has devoted his fortune to
the interest of the doctrines he professes. The Father,
Enfantin, has good sense and sound judgment upon
every other subject ; he regards seriously the mission
he believes to have received, and his followers appear
to consider it quite natural to show him respect and
submission. . . . The Pasha has employed those of the
Saint-Simonians whose services may be useful to him ;
they direct the works, and many of them, under M.
Linant, are engaged in the formation of a dam at the
Nile. M. Lambert has been placed at the head of a
school of mines, and he directs the working of a coal
mine at the foot of Lebanon ; no one is more capable
than he is to serve the interests of the Pasha in this
important branch. Other Saint-Simonians of different

professions live at Cairo, and support themselves by 1834.
various industries. . . . They have no more meetings
nor lectures. . . . Nothing distinguishes them now
from other people, except the dress they wear, and the
resignation they exhibit in their countenances. They
have shown much sense in adopting Egypt for their
residence; it is a country where they can be useful
and where they can live in peace." [85]

Towards the close of the year the works began to
languish; the necessities of agriculture had obliged
many to return to their homes, and only 1500 men remained. The appearance of the cholera shortly afterwards caused these to disperse also, and the project
was thus necessarily abandoned for the present. Enfantin and many other fugitives took refuge at Cairo,
where, however, the pestilence soon followed them.
The Father had the pain of seeing one after another of
his disciples fall victims to it,—first Fourcade, then
Busco, Lamé, Maréchal, and Alric, the sculptor; some
of these had contracted the disease at the hospitals,
where they had gone to render assistance, but a panic
rapidly spread among the population, and all who had
the means of flight left. Among them, Enfantin,
accompanied by Lambert, took the opportunity of
going up the Nile, and settled for a time at Carnac;
he subsequently pursued his journey alone to Thebes.
Ample time was thus afforded him for melancholy re-

[85] 'Œuvres,' vol. x. p. 60.

1835.   flection. He had left his disciples partly because his presence had become unacceptable. "I find here," he writes, "what I came to seek—isolation from a world in which my presence has become useless and often injurious; I was tired to find myself so frequently an obstacle when I wished only to be of service, and to rouse susceptibilities when I sought but for affection. The necessity for constant diplomacy exhausted all the forces of my body and mind." The failure of his expedition to Egypt was indeed complete: the female Messiah had not responded to his appeal; the industrial works that had so largely contributed to attract him to the East were abandoned. Many of his disciples had returned to France; those who remained were day by day succumbing to a terrible disease; the few who escaped had found employment in various ways, but not upon a scale at all answering to the magnificent anticipations of Enfantin.

In the midst of the dejection into which he was thrown by these misfortunes, the news reached him of the death of his father. The old man had not shared the enthusiasm of his son; he was disappointed to find a life that might have been devoted to retrieving the fortunes of the family, wasted upon unprofitable dreams. He could little understand the devotion that volunteered to labour, and rejected remuneration. The most serious trial Enfantin had to endure was the conflict that perpetually recurred between his duty and his affections.

The mission he was called upon to fulfil summoned 1835. him to lead his disciples to a distant land, far removed from his father's home. He had to resist the plaintive appeal of the old man who felt that he would never see him again. "C'en est donc fait pour cette fois, mon bon Prosper, je vais donc vous perdre pour toujours : c'est bien pour toujours : je ne m'abuse pas, je suis trop âgée pour espérer vous revoir jamais ; je n'ai rien à vous dire, puisque la voix de la nature n'a pas pu se faire entendre ; moi je ne peux que prier Dieu qu'il conduise vos pas et qu'il vous protége dans toutes vos grandes entreprises." [86] It is easy to imagine the effect such a letter was likely to produce upon a man who owed the influence he exercised over his disciples to the love his affectionate nature excited in their hearts. The stinging reproach penetrated deeply, and Enfantin wrote with some bitterness from Alexandria, "My father will very imperfectly understand how it is that I should prefer my position of a volunteer to receiving pay nearly equal to that enjoyed by Fournel. He will understand it all the less, because a salary would enable me to add some comforts to his existence; and he will think that I have again sacrificed a duty to what he considers a folly, but to what I consider to be a duty still more imperious." [87] But these complaints were now silenced for ever, and there followed many a solemn hour when the reproachful

[86] 'Œuvres,' vol. ix. p. 86.   [87] Ib. p. 237.

1836. face of the lonely old man haunted his still lonelier son
among the ruins at Thebes. Nothing but the confidence he had felt in himself and in his mission, could
have given him strength to resist the power of affection and to challenge the opinion of the world, and
now at the moment of his sorest need that confidence
deserted him. " Aujourd'hui," he wrote, " cette foi
en moi est épuisée, quant à mon action sur le monde."
Later in the year the death of Hoart completed his
discouragement. Hoart had been a captain of artillery,
and was the most energetic disciple left to the faith ;
he had greatly overtaxed his strength during the
summer, and he succumbed in the autumn to dysentery.
Enfantin and Bruneau were present at his death-bed,
and they both acknowledge that his loss was irre-
parable. With him all attempts to continue a collective apostleship terminated ; the disciples who remained returned to the world and adopted once more
its customs, and Enfantin remarked that the prophecy
of D'Eichthal at Ménilmontant was fulfilled, and that
he was left alone. He had never shown any hesitation
to depend for his support upon the subscriptions of his
followers. A friend of his, M. Arlès-Dufour, who was
largely engaged in commerce at Lyons, and who is now
widely known throughout Europe, proposed to relieve
him from this dependent position, by giving him an appointment as traveller in the East for the firm ; but
Enfantin rejected this offer with some asperity, as one

totally unsuited to his disposition. He, however, did _{to} 1836 to Dec. 1839.
not find any difficulty in accepting money from his
friend, and through this means he was able to return
to France at the close of 1836. For three years longer
he lived entirely upon charity. Sometimes he visited
his relation General Saint-Cyr, and found his health
greatly improved by cultivating the general's garden;
sometimes a disciple offered to share his fortune with
him. When Ribes heard that he intended to come to
Montpellier, he begged him not to attract attention by
wearing any fantastic costume. "But I am anxious,"
he wrote, "that those who formed what we called the
Saint-Simonian family should give you a material support not wholly unworthy of you. In the meantime
you may count upon the half of my income; we will
divide it regularly every month." [88] The hopes of
Ribes were realized by the energy of Arlès, and
Enfantin finally enjoyed what he called his "civil
list," a fund subscribed by a few faithful disciples,
and of which Holstein acted for a time as treasurer.
Some of the Saint-Simonians had attained to good
positions in the world. Urbain was travelling in
Algeria as interpreter to the Duke of Orleans.
Fournel continued to be employed as a civil engineer

[88] 'Œuvres,' vol. x. p. 216. Notwithstanding M. Ribes' very generous
character, his life was threatened by a serious calamity. "Je crains bien
en effet," he writes, "de ne pouvoir sortir de l'impasse où je suis et de
finir d'une manière malheureuse (pour avoir quelque chose à faire) par
le mariage et la clientèle" (p. 218).

to the railway between Saint-Germain and Paris. He was afterwards appointed mining engineer-in-chief in Algeria. Péreire, Flachat, and D'Eichthal had speculated successfully in the Saint-Germain railway. Michel Chevalier still wrote in the 'Journal des Débats,' and in 1840 he succeeded Rossi as professor at the College of France. Rodrigue was speculating on the Bourse; Barrault was engaged upon the composition of a book; Duveyrier had produced a play called 'Le Monomane,' which was acted at the Porte Saint-Martin theatre; and Laurent had accepted a small legal appointment.

In the midst of all this, however, the faith did not prosper. The most zealous were dismayed by the dissensions which still agitated the church, and by the lukewarmness and apostasy of many in matters of doctrine. Even Enfantin himself maintained that the world had been sufficiently impressed by the exceptional life at Ménilmontant and elsewhere, and that the time had arrived when their interests would be better served by mixing freely with the world in the ordinary manner, and without any special efforts at conversion. He said that celibacy, costumes, and common property were necessary to be realized by apostles temporarily, for the benefit of posterity. It was an exalted superstition which has had its victims, but which was an important agent in attracting the attention of the world. Now, however, the Supreme Father of Ménilmontant

has fitly disappeared,—the future spouse of the female
Messiah has veiled his face. To give the more effect
to this determination, he accepted an appointment
upon a scientific commission then about to proceed to
Algeria. He arrived in the colony in December, 1839.
Five years later, the affairs of the Saint-Simonians were
finally wound up by the liquidation of their debts,
which still amounted to 60,000 francs.[89] For this purpose, a collection was made among those who were
formerly the most ardent disciples, and who had now
become prosperous men in the old world; the principal contributors were Madame Petit and M. Gustave
d'Eichthal.[90] What remains to be related belongs
more properly to the biography of Enfantin than to the
history of Saint-Simonism.

V.

Having spent two years (1840 and 1841) in Algeria,
Enfantin returned to France, where he resumed, for a
time, his dependent life. His relative, General Saint-
Cyr-Nugues, was always ready to offer him assistance;
it was to the influence of Saint-Cyr that Enfantin
owed his appointment in Algeria, and now, upon his
return, he lived chiefly with the general at Curson, near
Valence, on the Rhone. The Government offered to
give him an appointment as *sous-préfet*, but, notwith-

[89] ' Œuvres,' vol. vi. p. 229.

[90] Enfantin said that no less than one million of francs (£40,000)
had been spent upon the movement. (' Œuvres,' vol. v. p. 222.)

1845. standing his abject want, he indignantly declined.
He occupied his leisure by writing letters to the
king and to the Duke of Orleans, in which he freely
expressed his views on the political events of the day,
and also upon the composition of a work relating to
the 'Colonization of Algeria;' the latter, at first, assumed the form of a report, which he presented to
the Minister of War, but as that official declined to
receive it, it subsequently appeared as a book. These
literary pursuits were diversified by occasional visits to
former friends. At Paris he received the homage
society pays to fame, and made the acquaintance of
the leading statesmen and writers of the day. At
Meudon he again met the mother of his child Arthur;
that lady was very anxious to marry her former lover,
but Enfantin steadily declined, for "purely doctrinal
reasons." He says that he has retained his old habit
of judging his acts by placing himself 500 years in
advance of the age, and from that advanced point of
view marriage appears utterly foolish. He admits,
however, that the position of his mistress, amid the
prejudices of existing society, is not an enviable one;
and some of his former friends, who had been his disciples, urged him, on that account, but without success,
to marry her. Their son, Arthur, was brought up
and educated carefully as a civil engineer.

The construction of railways was at that time going
forward with great activity throughout France. By the

influence of Arlès, Enfantin obtained a seat in the council of administration of the Paris and Lyons Railway ; from that moment, to the hour of his death, he was placed in an independent position as regards money, and at one time he had even a prospect of acquiring a handsome fortune. He displayed considerable ability in his new occupation ; and it was in some degree due to his exertions that the lines between Paris and Marseilles were formed into a single company. As a reward for his services, he was sent to Lyons, in 1852, to represent the Council of Administration. While there, he was enabled to get his son an appointment, from which he has since risen to be the chief inspector of the line. Although Enfantin found many of his old friends at Lyons, among others, Arlès and Holstein, he was yet not sorry to be transferred to Paris, in 1856, where he continued to reside till his death. During the later years of his life he exhibited considerable aptitude for the practical affairs of the world ; but although he modified, he did not abandon, the theories of his youth. Of these, there was none he so fondly cherished as the construction of a canal between the Mediterranean and the Red Sea ; although his efforts had been unsuccessful during his visit to Egypt, he still clung to the idea. He conducted an extensive correspondence with a view of interesting Europe in the matter ; and it was to a great extent by his exertions that the " Société des Études " was

1846. founded at Paris, in 1846. The object of the society was to ascertain the probable cost of the canal, from investigations made upon the spot; it was composed of not more than thirty-three members. France, Austria, and England were equally represented, and each furnished one engineer. Capital to the amount of 150,000 francs was subscribed in three equal sums, and the society was to meet for deliberation on the first Monday of every month at the house of M. Enfantin, who was one of the members. The engineers that were chosen to represent their respective countries were MM. Talabot, Negrelli, and Stephenson. The first was appointed to survey the country through which the canal was to pass, and the other two were to report upon the harbours that would be required in the Mediterranean and the Red Sea.[91] The society received an assurance of support from the chambers of commerce at Lyons and Marseilles; some years, however, elapsed, before anything resulted. It was not till 1851, that Mr. Stephenson recommended the construction of a railway instead of a canal. His decision was

---

[91] " En 1846 un homme d'un incontestable talent qui a joué un rôle tout spécial dans le monde contemporain, M. Enfantin, inspira à quelques amis l'idée d'entreprendre à nouveau l'étude d'un projet de réunion des deux mers." The result was the formation of the 'Société des Études,' and the report of M. Talabot. " N'eût-il eu pour effets que de fournir l'occasion d'un nivellement exact entre les deux mers et de concentrer désormais les efforts vers un canal maritime direct, au lieu d'un tracé indirect avec alimentation par le Nil, qu'on lui devrait déjà une mention à part."—*Ritt. Hist. de l'Isthme de Suez*, p. 100.

attributed to national jealousy, and it was regarded by some of his colleagues as a new instance of English perfidy. A railway, they said, would be of great service to England, but of little either to France or Austria. At all events, the "Société des Études" had expended 120,000 francs, and it was to a great degree in consequence of the investigation it had made that Mr. Stephenson had been able to form his opinion. Enfantin, therefore, maintained that Stephenson should either include the members of the "Société" in the advantages to be derived from the railway, or else repay to the German and French groups the share they had contributed to the funds of the association. An angry correspondence followed. "Do you think," asks Enfantin, in one of his letters, " do you really think that Stephenson considers, as he said, that the canal was impossible? Such a word does not belong to the vocabulary of that great engineer, scarcely to the English language; for the English do miracles in industry where other nations cry 'It is impossible!'"[92] Enfantin was not the only member of the "Société des Études" who was indignant at the conduct of Stephenson. M. Negrelli, the Austrian engineer, acknowledged that "he would be delighted if we could give a check to Stephenson, for he has behaved throughout like a true Englishman."[93] Towards the close of 1854, a valuable auxiliary was obtained in M. de Lesseps, who, it will

[92] 'Œuvres,' vol. xii. p. 220.   [93] Ib. p. 223.

1854. be remembered, was not unacquainted with Enfantin. During his consulship at Cairo, De Lesseps had been upon intimate terms with Saïd Pasha, at whose request he was now about to return to Egypt. On his way from Paris he had an interview at Lyons with MM. Enfantin and Arlès, and at Marseilles with M. Talabot. These gentlemen provided him with all the documents that were necessary to interest the Pasha in the construction of a canal, and to afford him the information required for its execution. M. de Lesseps succeeded in his negotiation, and communicated the result to Arlès; he also sent a copy of his report to the Viceroy, and of the firman of concession, but he deferred, he said, till his return to France, to enter into details. "We will then arrange together the definitive basis of our great enterprise; in the meantime, however, I think you may fitly begin now to make whatever overtures, and to take whatever steps you may deem necessary."[94] But there unhappily arose a difference of opinion between De Lesseps and Arlès, as to the route the canal should take. "I regret," wrote the former, "that M. Arlès-Dufour should have persisted, in spite of my observations, to advocate a project of which the Viceroy does not approve. I have informed him from the beginning that Mohamed Saïd Pasha pronounced at once against the route suggested by M. Talabot, and which is cer-

[94] 'Œuvres,' vol. xii. p. 229.

tainly not without merit."[95]   The result of this unfortunate dispute was that M. de Lesseps was, for the
future, enabled to act quite independently of MM.
Arlès, Enfantin, and Talabot, who represented the
"Société des Études."   Accordingly, when the company was formed for the execution of the project, to
the study of which these gentlemen had devoted so
much energy, they found themselves altogether excluded.   It was expected that Enfantin would have
made a vigorous remonstrance, but he disinterestedly
remarked that, "Provided the work which I have
brought into notice, and caused to be studied as highly
useful to the moral and material interests of humanity,
be executed, I will be the first to bless him by whom
it is executed.   Undoubtedly, it is but just that posterity should know that the initiation of that gigantic
enterprise was taken by those whom the old world
could recognise only as utopists, dreamers, or fools,—
but we appeal to history for our vindication; in the
meantime, if the isthmus be cut, although not by us, it
will belong especially to us to cry Allah-Kérim."[96]

In this manner Enfantin practised an essential doctrine of his faith, that labour in the interests of humanity is a religious duty, and, as such, is its own
sufficient reward.   At the same time he continued to
propagate his views by means of the press, so far as
other occupations would allow.   In 1839 Vinçard

[95] 'Œuvres,' vol. xii. p. 234.   [96] Ib. p. 248.

started a paper, called 'La Ruche Populaire,' to which
Raymond Bonheur contributed; it was an organ of
the working classes, and endeavoured to diffuse the
doctrines of Saint-Simonism among the centres of
communistic propagation then existing in the principal towns of France. It was succeeded, in 1843, by
'L'Union, bulletin des Ouvriers,' and early in the following year 'L'Algérie' was begun by Enfantin, with
the assistance of Louis Jourdan, and two members of
the late Commission. It was not, however, till after
the revolution in 1848 that Saint-Simonism could
make any efforts in journalism. Enfantin had then
acquired a considerable fortune, and was better able
to support the expenses of a newspaper. Duveyrier
undertook to edit 'Le Crédit.' "I wish," he said, "to
be one of those who are about to begin, with the full
consciousness of the dignity of the work, to prepare
for the reign of God." Enfantin contributed many
articles to the new paper, and invested a large part of
his fortune in the undertaking. He fancied that it
would be a commercial success, but in this he was disappointed; after an existence of two years it ceased to
appear, having entailed a loss of upwards of £7000. It
had sought to oppose the revolutionary socialism advocated by 'La Vraie République,' 'La Démocratie,' and
'Le Peuple,' and which were supported by such men
as Victor Considérant and Ledru Rollin. 'Le Crédit'
was patronized by Cavaignac; Dufaure, Marrast, and

Lamartine had pronounced it to be an "admirable 1848. journal." It was succeeded by a weekly review, 'La Politique Nouvelle,' conducted by Lhabitant, and in which Enfantin and Laurent wrote.[97]

In addition to these literary occupations, Enfantin found time to edit his 'Correspondance Philosophique et Religieuse,' which he published in 1847. This work was followed in 1858 by 'La Science de l'Homme, Physiologie Religieuse,' which he dedicated to the late Emperor, and in 1861 by 'La Vie Éternelle.' He also undertook to contribute to an Encyclopedia which Gide was about to publish. Michel Chevalier wrote the prospectus, and some of the most eminent men in France were associated in the undertaking. The names of Guizot, Thiers, Villemain, Littré, Lamartine, and Renan occur in the same list along with those of Fournel, Lambert, Duveyrier, and Enfantin.[98] The last scheme of the old theorist was intended to benefit those classes who are engaged in literature, science, and art : he proposed that the students in these various departments who had given proof of ability at college, should be considered thereby to have afforded a guarantee of future success, so that a purely financial company would be justified in advancing sufficient capital to enable the young men to prosecute their studies at leisure. He asks why Fulton, or Watt, or

[97] 'Œuvres,' vol. xi. pp. 192, 212 ; vol. xii. pp. 89, 123, 128, 135, 146, 166, 179, 181.

[98] 'Œuvres,' vol. xii. pp. 65–69 ; vol. xiii. pp. 34, 60, 119.

1863. David after the rehearsal of the 'Désert,' or Molière, or Corneille, or Racine, should be obliged to go about to beg for patronage from a prince. Have not the scholars whose names appear among the first ten at the final examination at the Polytechnic School established their title to receive credit in virtue of their brains, not as an act of charity, but as a purely commercial speculation? The money would of course be lent on the principle of mutual guarantee, such as has been introduced into Germany by M. Schulze-Delitzsch; the only difference being that in this case it is lent to brains instead of to hands. The same care would be taken to investigate the character of each individual, and to obtain a satisfactory proof of his capacity. "The names," he said, "of the labourers in science and art are not yet inscribed in the books of the bank, credit does not exist for them; it is for you to give it to them."[99] The 'Crédit Intellectuel' received some influential support: M. de Jouvencel wrote a pamphlet in its favour; the 'Moniteur' declared that whatever difficulties the scheme might present, it was not impracticable; Arlès advocated it strongly. A commission was appointed to investigate the matter; they met several times, but their decision was unfavourable. The opposition consisted of MM. Michel Chevalier, Duveyrier, and Péreire, and the discussion was carried on with so much warmth, that it unfortunately led to a quarrel

[99] 'Œuvres,' vol. xiii. p. 178.

1864.

between them and Enfantin. This was the more to be regretted, because for thirty years they had been united through good and evil report, and now but one year of life remained to him whom they had once followed and called "Father" and "Master." For some time past Enfantin had been highly prosperous; his occupation upon the Lyons Railway afforded him a competency sufficient for his wants, and yet left him ample leisure to pursue his favourite studies. He had secured a certain amount of fame, and now he enjoyed its privilege,—the society of eminent men. But his health began to fail, and he had to renounce the dinner-parties and assemblies in which he had so long delighted. He withdrew without repining, to spend the few months that remained to him in comparative solitude, meditating upon that eternal life of which he had so long dreamed, and surrounded by only a few of his most intimate friends, in whom he had inspired his own faith. "My body," he says, "is getting weak, my beard is long and white, my hand trembles, but my mind is still clear, and my heart warm." Although his disease had been of long standing, the end came unexpectedly. He was preparing to go on a fishing expedition with his friend and disciple Laurent, when he was attacked by acute symptoms, to which he succumbed in a few days. He died on the 31st August, 1864, in the 69th year of his age, and was buried at Père-la-Chaise, near to his master, Saint-Simon. His

1864. funeral was largely attended, and among others by his son Arthur, by Arlès, d'Eichthal, Duveyrier, Fournel, Laurent, Barrault, David, and by many whose names are intimately associated with his. He bequeathed a portion of his fortune to literary executors, for the purpose of publishing his papers, and an account of his life; and it is to their labours that we owe the collection from which I have compiled the preceding narrative. Before his death he transferred the whole of his library and manuscripts to the Bibliothèque de l'Arsenal, of which Saint-Simon had once been for a short time the librarian. The papers of Fourier and Barrier, and those of Robinet, the disciple of Comte, are also deposited there, where it is proposed to assemble a curious collection of works on Sociology. Enfantin had the satisfaction of witnessing some of his disciples attain to eminent positions in the world, where their talents could be usefully employed. Michel Chevalier, who is perhaps the most eminent, filled the chair of Political Economy at the Collége de France for many years. His lectures have been described as an eloquent and profound exposition of whatever is best in Saint-Simonism, freed from the errors which youth and inexperience had associated with its first essays.[100] He was returned to the Chamber of Deputies in 1845 for L'Aveyron, and soon became known in France as the leading advocate of free trade, and the uncompromising op-

[100] 'Œuvres,' vol. xi. p. 160.

ponent of Protection. He was for many years the friend of Mr. Cobden, with whom he actively co-operated. He attained finally to the rank of Senator, under the late Empire, and he continues to be, in the language of Cobden, "the friend of every man who wishes for progress, and the enlightenment and prosperity of mankind."[101]

David, whose youthful genius was devoted to the composition of chants for the Saint-Simonian worship, and whose melodies echoed along the shores of the Levant and in the concert-halls of Alexandria and Cairo, has since then secured a permanent fame in Europe. His great operas, 'Le Désert' and 'Herculanum,' were received with enthusiasm at Paris; and, in 1867, he obtained the prize of 20,000 francs which is awarded every ten years to the author of the best opera during the interval.

Raymond Bonheur has left a legacy which will entitle him to the enduring remembrance of posterity. The reader may, perhaps, recollect his passionate confession of love and admiration for the gentler sex, and the ardent desire he expressed to compass their deliverance from the social disabilities under which they labour. His daughter, Rosa Bonheur, who may justly claim to be among the greatest of living artists, and whose works will bear comparison with the greatest of the past, has established beyond dis-

1864.

[101] 'Speeches,' vol. ii. p. 327.

1864.   pute the capacity of women to perform work of supreme excellence,—a fact which had been hitherto frequently contested.

After the revolution in 1848, some of the disciples found seats in the Constituent Assembly, and rose to political importance; among these were Laurent, Reynaud, and Charton. Duveyrier, who had been called the poet of God, and who composed the words to which David supplied the music, had become an influential journalist, and he wrote a pamphlet which at the time attacted much attention. It was called 'L'Empereur François-Joseph et l'Europe.' Barrault, who had been the most eloquent advocate of Saint-Simonism in its early days, was also its most faithful disciple. When the others had become lukewarm, and when even Enfantin was engrossed with worldly affairs, Barrault quitted Paris for Algeria to found an agricultural colony on Saint-Simonian principles; he started in October, 1849, accompanied by 800 to 1000 persons. Enfantin assisted him with money, though he had little faith in the success of the undertaking. He had, indeed, recommended the establishment of colonies, but his scheme required to be executed upon a large scale, and modelled, in regard to discipline, upon the military system. " In the army," he remarks, " gradations in rank and authority are already established, while in civil life that is precisely what is wanting; and in an enterprise conducted upon the principle of association, a central administra-

1864.

tion is imperiously required."[102] The agricultural association of Algeria, such as Barrault attempted to form, would only serve to show more clearly the necessity of totally changing the present order of society, by introducing once more the principle of authority. "Every such isolated attempt," Enfantin wrote, "is what Ménilmontant was,—an eccentricity, a society outside of society, an apostleship,—and, notwithstanding all you say about my inability to modify my opinions, I have not the slightest wish to begin that over again."[103] We are not informed as to the result of Barrault's efforts, but if it had been triumphant, it is not likely that it would have remained unrecorded. For many years past Enfantin discouraged any such attempts; he considered that the true method of acquiring influence in the world is by mixing freely in it, and by the quiet and unostentatious statement of opinions. Nor was he at all disposed to fancy that he and his followers were its only valuable members, or that their opinions embraced all that was important. On the contrary, he reproved a disciple for undue pride. "You are," he said, "by far too disposed to despise those who do not belong to us; for my own part, I believe that there are many who are not only quite as good, but even better, although they never lived in the Rue Monsigny or at Ménil-

[102] 'Œuvres,' vol. xi. p. 199.
[103] 'Œuvres,' vol. xii. p. 120.

montaut." He could not conceal the dislike with which he regarded the various socialist sects that sprang up in 1848. They violated the two principles he deemed especially sacred,—the principle of authority, and the principle of reward according to capacity and merit. But if he derived little satisfaction from that quarter, and refused to recognise the analogy between their innovations and his own, he fancied he saw in the world about him the influence of the opinions he had so long advocated. The effort towards the establishment of free trade was, he fondly hoped, the commencement of a peaceful association among nations; and the union that arose among workmen in various countries was the first symptom of that universal brotherhood which is to replace the feuds of bygone centuries. He was fortunately spared the pain of witnessing the fearful tragedy that has recently been enacted in Europe, and which has so sadly shown how far civilization is yet removed from its final triumph over the ferocious passions of barbarism. He pointed to the exertions that had been successfully made to diffuse education among the lowest and poorest classes, and the thousand efforts to ameliorate their condition by the multiplication of friendly and co-operative societies, and the extension of credit to labour. He hailed with enthusiasm the appearance of the champions of the rights of woman in nearly every part of the world, and the partial success that has already rewarded their labours. It is ^{1864.} true that his eyes were never destined to behold the female Messiah, but with the many evidences around him of the working of his Master's spirit, he could sink into his silent grave in peace, with the confident hope that when his dust shall have returned to its kindred elements, and his memory has long since perished, his spirit will yet survive, though transformed and ineffably feeble, in the large inheritance the future will have to acknowledge from the past.

THE END.

APPENDICES.

APPENDICES.

———•———

No. 1, *page* 67.

"Nos pères se sont abusés en croyant qu'ils avaient une grande force de raisonnement . . . ils ont basé leur système scientifique sur un produit indigeste de leur imagination."—*Œuvres Choisies*, 1808, vol. i. p. 185.

"Dans le commencement des travaux astronomiques, l'homme *mêlait* les faits qu'il *observait* avec ceux qu'il *imaginait*; et dans ce galimatias élémentaire, il faisait les meilleures combinaisons qu'il pouvait pour satisfaire toutes les demandes de prédiction."—*Lettres de Genève*, 1803.

Compare M. Comte ('Politique Positive,' 1822, App. vol. iv. p. 77) :—" Dans le premier [état], des idées surnaturelles servent à lier le petit nombre d'observations isolées dont la science se compose alors. En d'autres termes, les faits observés sont *expliqués*, c'est-à-dire, vus *à priori*, d'après des faits inventés. Cet état est nécessairement celui de toute science au berceau."

No. 2, *page* 67.

"Les sciences ont commencé par être conjecturales, parce qu'à l'origine des travaux scientifiques il n'y avait

encore que peu d'observations faites, que le petit nombre de
celles qui avaient été faites n'avaient pas eu le temps d'être
examinées, discutées, vérifiées par une longue expérience,
et que ce n'étaient que des faits présumés, des conjectures."
—M. Burdin's views, quoted and endorsed by Saint-Simon,
Œuvres Choisies, 1818, vol. ii. p. 21.

M. Comte, in his earliest writings, alluded to the same
period by the same name :—" La supériorité," he says, " du
positif sur le conjectural, de la physique sur la métaphysique." Again, " Le pouvoir spirituel étant de sa nature
conjectural."—*Pol. Pos.* App. vol. iv. pp. 7, 8.

" A l'époque où toutes nos connaissances particulières
étaient essentiellement conjecturales et métaphysiques, il
était naturel que la direction de la société, quant à ses
affaires spirituelles, fût entre les mains d'un pouvoir théologique, puisque les théologiens étaient alors les seuls métaphysiciens généraux. . . . La capacité scientifique positive
est très-supérieure à la théologie et à la métaphysique."—
Comte, *Ib.* 1820, p. 7.

No. 3, *page* 67.

" Le système religieux a été d'abord l'Idolâtrie, c'est-à-
dire, la croyance que les premières causes étaient visibles, et
l'adoration de ces causes par ceux qui ne travaillaient pas
à étudier la relation des causes et des effets et à en perfectionner la connaissance. Que de l'idée de causes visibles,
l'homme s'est élevé à l'idée de plusieurs causes invisibles et
animées, ce qui a constitué le Polythéisme. Que de l'idée
de plusieurs causes invisibles et animées, l'homme s'est
élevé à l'idée d'une seule cause invisible et animée, ce qui a
constitué le Déisme."—*Œuvres Choisies* 1813, vol. ii. p. 34.

" Les Égyptiens ont adoré les astres, les fleuves, les montagnes, certains végétaux, quelques animaux. . . . Ainsi en science générale, l'esprit humain a commencé par croire à l'existence d'un grand nombre de causes indépendantes. Il a adopté ensuite l'idée de plusieurs causes considérées comme fraction d'un même tout—l'Intelligence. Il s'est élevé, après, à l'idée d'une intelligence universelle et unique —Dieu."—*Œuvres Choisies*, 1808, vol. i. p. 199.

No. 4, *page 67.*

" Les hommes ont senti plus tard que le désordre règnerait dans l'univers si plusieurs causes indépendantes, comme on l'avait imaginé jusque là, étaient chargées de régir le monde, et ils se sont élevés à l'idée d'une cause première unique."— *Ib.* 1813, vol. ii. p. 102.

No. 5, *page 67.*

"Socrate ensuite conçut l'idée de former un être composé de la réunion de tous ceux créés par Homère. Il inventa Dieu. Ce philosophe enseigna à ses disciples que les hommes devaient considérer tout ce qui existait comme étant le résultat d'une seule cause."—*Ib.* 1808, vol. i. p. 206.

No. 6, *page 67.*

" L'opinion de Socrate s'était répandue; elle avait été adoptée par tous les hommes éclairés, lorsque Jésus parut. . . . Il fonda la religion chrétienne, à laquelle il donna le déisme pour base."—*Ib.* 1808, vol. i. p. 207.

No. 7, *page* 67.

"Les Européens, formant l'avant-garde scientifique de l'espèce humaine, ont suivi la direction donnée par Socrate, jusqu'au moment où les Arabes ont imaginé de chercher les lois qui régissent l'univers, en faisant abstraction de l'idée d'une cause animée le gouvernant."—*Œuvres Choisies*, 1813, vol. ii. p. 53. Cf. 1808, vol. i. p. 195; and M. Comte: "L'introduction des sciences positives en Europe par les Arabes a créé le germe de cette importante révolution."—*Pol. Pos.* 1820, vol. iv. App. p. 7.

No. 8, *page* 68.

"A mesure que l'organisation du système de physique a avancé, les savants ont été déistes moins chauds. La chaleur de leur croyance en Dieu a continuellement diminué. Mais elle n'est pas encore totalement éteinte. . . . Les savants avaient trois conditions à remplir pour être en mesure d'abandonner complétement le déisme. 1° Celle de trouver une idée simple qui pût servir de base au système de physique. Newton a rempli cette première condition en trouvant l'idée de la gravitation. 2° Celle de vérifier l'exactitude de l'idée, du fait ou du principe trouvé. . . . 3° Celle de lier l'idée, le fait ou le principe général trouvé, avec les idées, les faits ou les principes du second ordre de généralité."—*Œuvres Choisies*, 1808, vol. i. p. 229.

No. 9, *page* 68.

Man "a enfin senti que les relations entre Dieu et l'univers étant incompréhensibles et indifférentes (indifférentes, puisque Dieu, ayant prévu tout ce qui arriverait, ne peut rien changer à l'ordre qu'il a établi), il devait s'attacher à la recherche des faits, et considérer le fait le plus général qu'il découvrirait, comme cause unique de tous les phénomènes."—*Œuvres Choisies*, 1808, vol. i. p. 200.   And again, " Que de l'idée d'une seule cause invisible et animée, l'homme s'est élevé à la conception de plusieurs lois régissant les diverses classes de phénomènes.   Que l'homme s'élèvera à la croyance d'une seule et unique loi régissant l'univers (ce qui constituera l'avenir)."—*Œuvres Choisies*, 1813, vol. ii. p. 34.

No. 10, *page* 68.

". . . La pesanteur universelle : elle est la loi unique à laquelle j'ai soumis l'univers."—*Lettres de Genève*, 1808. These words are supposed to be uttered by an apparition of God.

No. 11, *page* 68.

" L'idée d'une loi générale régissant l'univers est à celle de plusieurs lois particulières réglant les phénomènes des diverses branches de la Physique, comme celle d'un seul Dieu à celle du Polythéisme."—*Science de l'Homme, Œuvres Choisies*, 1813, vol. ii. p. 122.   Compare Comte : " Le système théologique est parvenu à la plus haute perfection dont il soit susceptible, quand il a substitué l'action providentielle d'un être unique au jeu varié des nombreuses divinités indépendantes qui avaient été imaginées primitivement.   De même, le dernier terme du système métaphysique consiste à concevoir, au lieu des différentes entités particulières, une seule grande entité générale, la *nature*, envisagée comme la source unique de tous les phénomènes.   Pareille-

R

ment, la perfection du système positif, vers laquelle il tend sans cesse, quoiqu'il soit très-probable qu'il ne doive jamais l'atteindre, serait de pouvoir se représenter tous les divers phénomènes observables comme des cas particuliers d'un seul fait général, tel que celui de la gravitation, par exemple."—*Cours de Phil. Positive*, ed. Littré, vol. i. p. 10.

No. 12, *page* 68.

"En examinant le caractère relatif et positif du tout et des parties de la science, on trouve que le tout et les parties ont dû commencer par avoir le caractère conjectural; qu'ensuite le tout et les parties ont dû avoir le caractère mi-conjectural et positif; qu'enfin le tout et les parties doivent acquérir, autant que possible, le caractère positif. Nous en sommes au point que le premier bon résumé des sciences particulières constituera la philosophie positive. Il a été jusqu'à présent impossible de faire un bon système de philosophie: il est possible aujourd'hui de réussir dans cette entreprise; mais cela n'est pas aisé, cela est même fort difficile."—*Œuvres*, 1811, vol. xvii. p. 109.

No. 13, *page* 69.

"Les premiers phénomènes que l'homme ait observés d'une manière suivie ont été les phénomènes astronomiques. Il y a une bonne raison pour qu'il ait commencé par ceux-là : c'est qu'ils sont plus simples."—*Lettres de Genève*, 1803 ; *Hubbard*, p. 133.

No. 14, *page* 69.

"L'astronomie, étant la science dans laquelle on envisage les faits sous les rapports les plus simples et les moins nombreux, est la première qui doit avoir acquis le caractère positif. La chimie doit avoir marché après l'astronomie et avant la physiologie, parce qu'elle considère l'action de la matière sous des rapports plus compliqués que la première, mais moins détaillés que la physiologie."—*Œuvres Choisies*, 1818, vol. ii. p. 21.

"La tendance (de l'esprit humain) depuis cette époque (xv⁰ siècle) est de baser tous ses raisonnements sur des faits observés et discutés; déjà il a réorganisé sur cette base positive l'Astronomie, la Physique et la Chimie. . . . On conclut de là nécessairement que la physiologie, dont la science de l'homme fait partie, sera traitée par la méthode adoptée pour les autres sciences physiques, et qu'elle sera introduite dans l'instruction publique quand elle aura été rendue positive."—*Ib.* 1813, vol. ii. p. 14.

Compare Comte (*Pol. Pos.* 1820, vol. iv. App. p. 82): —"Les sciences sont successivement devenues positives dans l'ordre naturel qu'elles devaient suivre pour cela, c'est-à-dire, dans celui du degré plus ou moins grand de leurs rapports avec l'homme. C'est ainsi que l'astronomie d'abord, la physique ensuite, plus tard la chimie, et de nos jours enfin la physiologie, ont été constituées sciences positives." And again: "Les sciences sont devenues positives l'une après l'autre, dans l'ordre où il était naturel que cette révolution s'opérât. Cet ordre est celui du degré de complication plus ou moins grand de leurs phénomènes, ou, en d'autres termes, de leur rapport plus ou moins intime avec l'homme. Ainsi les phénomènes astronomiques d'abord, comme étant les plus simples, et ensuite successivement les physiques, les chimiques et les physiologiques, ont été ramenés à des théories positives; ceux-ci à une époque toute récente. La même réforme ne pouvait s'effectuer qu'en dernier lieu pour les phénomènes politiques, qui sont les plus compliqués puisqu'ils dépendent de tous les autres."—1822, p. 80.

No. 15, *page* 69.

" La physiologie se trouve encore dans la mauvaise position par laquelle ont passé les sciences astrologiques [evidently a misprint for 'astronomiques'] et chimiques. Il faut que les physiologistes chassent de leur société les *philosophes*, les *moralistes* et les *métaphysiciens*, comme les astronomes ont chassé les astrologues, comme les chimistes ont chassé les alchimistes."—*Lettres de Genève*, 1803, Hubbard, p. 134. See also *Œuvres Choisies*, 1813, vol. ii. p. 14.

" La physiologie ne mérite pas encore d'être classée au nombre des sciences positives ; mais elle n'a plus qu'un seul pas à faire pour s'élever complétement au-dessus de l'ordre des sciences conjecturales."—*Ib*. 1813, vol. ii. p. 22.

No. 16, *page* 69.

" La physiologie, qui pendant longtemps a nagé dans le charlatanisme, se base aujourd'hui sur des faits observés et discutés. La psychologie commence à se baser sur la physiologie, et à se débarrasser des préjugés religieux, sur lesquels elle était fondée."—*Ib*. p. 21. M. Burdin quoted and approved by Saint-Simon.

No. 17, *page* 70.

" Vous ne trouverez point aux phénomènes que vous avez appelés *moraux* et à ceux que vous avez appelés physiques un caractère différent."—*Lettres de Genève*, 1803 ; *Hubbard*, p. 145.

"La matière existe sous deux formes ; forme solide et forme fluide : . . . la pensée est une attraction matérielle ; elle est un résultat du mouvement du fluide nerveux."— *Œuvres Choisies*, 1808, vol. i. pp. 166, 170.

No. 18, *page* 70.

" L'homme n'a pas été primitivement séparé des autres animaux par une forte ligne de démarcation. . . . Sa structure . . . est la plus avantageuse de toutes. Pourquoi attribuer sa supériorité morale à une autre cause ? La ligne de démarcation entre l'intelligence de l'homme et l'instinct des animaux, n'a été clairement tracée qu'après la formation du système des signes de convention parlés ou écrits."—*Ib.* 1808, vol. i. p. 171.

" Si la différence est immense aujourd'hui entre l'intelligence de l'homme et celle des autres animaux, c'est par la raison que l'homme s'est placé, dès la première génération, dans la position la plus avantageuse pour son perfectionnement."—*Ib.* 1808, p. 172.

Compare M. Comte :—"La supériorité de l'homme sur les autres animaux ne pouvant avoir et n'ayant, en effet, d'autre cause que la perfection relative de son organisation, tout ce qu'a fait l'espèce humaine et tout ce qu'elle peut faire, doit évidemment être regardé, en dernière analyse, comme une conséquence nécessaire de son organisation modifiée dans ses effets par l'état de l'extérieure."—*Comte, op. cit.* 1822, p. 125.

No. 19, *page* 70.

" Mes amis, nous sommes des corps organisés : c'est en considérant comme phénomènes physiologiques nos relations sociales que j'ai conçu le projet que je vous présente."— *Lettres de Genève*, 1803.

"La politique générale, qui comprend le système religieux et l'organisation du clergé, ne sera une science positive qu'à l'époque où la philosophie sera devenue, dans toutes ses parties, une science d'observation ; car la politique générale est une application de la science générale."—*Œuvres Choisies*, 1813, vol. ii. p. 16.

"La morale deviendra une science positive."—*Ib.* 1813, vol. ii. p. 23.

"La politique deviendra une science positive."—*Ib.*

"Que la politique deviendrait une science d'observation, et que les questions politiques seraient un jour traitées par ceux qui auraient étudié la science positive de l'homme, par la même méthode et de la même manière qu'on traite aujourd'hui celles relatives aux autres phénomènes."—*Ib.* 1813, vol. ii. p. 147. Compare p. 152.

"Sire, les progrès de l'esprit humain sont arrivés à ce point où les raisonnements les plus importants sur la politique peuvent et doivent être directement déduits des connaissances acquises dans les hautes sciences et dans les sciences physiques. Donner à la politique un caractère positif est l'objet de mon ambition."—*Ib.* 1813, vol. ii. p. 174.

"La méthode des sciences d'observation doit être appliquée à la politique : le raisonnement et l'expérience sont les éléments de cette méthode."—*Ib.* 1814, p. 285.

No. 20, *page* 70.

"La religion est la collection des applications de la science générale."—*Ib.* 1808, vol. i. p. 213.

No. 21, *page* 70.

"On voit que les sciences particulières sont les éléments

de la science générale ; que la science générale, c'est-à-dire
la philosophie, a dû être conjecturale, tant que les sciences
particulières l'ont été ; qu'elle a dû être mi-conjecturale et
positive, quand une partie des sciences particulières est
devenue positive, pendant que l'autre était encore conjecturale, et qu'elle sera tout-à-fait positive quand toutes les
sciences particulières le seront—ce qui arrivera à l'époque
où la physiologie et la psychologie seront basées sur des
faits observés et discutés ; car il n'existe pas de phénomène
qui ne soit astronomique, chimique, physiologique, ou psy-
chologique. On a donc connaissance d'une époque à laquelle la philosophie qui sera enseignée dans les écoles sera
positive."—*Œuvres Choisies*, 1813, vol. ii. p. 15.

No. 22, *page* 70.

"Dupuis a démontré jusqu'à l'évidence . . . que toutes
les religions connues ont été fondées sur le système scientifique, et que toute réorganisation du système scientifique
entraînait par conséquent réorganisation et amélioration du
système religieux."—*Ib.* 1813, vol. ii. p. 24.

No. 23, *page* 71.

"On voit que les systèmes de religion, de politique générale, de morale, d'instruction publique, ne sont autre chose
que des applications du système des idées. . . . Ainsi il est
évident qu'après la confection du nouveau système scientifique, il y aura réorganisation des systèmes de religion,
de politique générale, de morale, d'instruction publique,
et que par conséquent le clergé sera réorganisé."—*Œuvres
Choisies*, 1813, vol. ii. p. 15. Compare *ib.* p. 133.

No. 24, *page* 71.

" Je crois à la nécessité d'une religion pour le maintien
de l'ordre social ; je crois que le déisme est usé ; je crois
que le physicisme n'est point assez solidement établi pour
pouvoir servir de base à une religion.   Je crois que la torce
des choses veut qu'il y ait deux doctrines distinctes : le Physicisme pour les gens instruits, et le Déisme pour la classe
ignorante."—*Ib.* 1808, vol. i. p. 214.

" La philosophie deviendra une science positive. . . . La
science générale, ou philosophie, a pour faits élémentaires
les faits généraux des sciences particulières, qui sont les
éléments de la science générale."—*Ib.* 1813, vol. ii. p. 23.
Compare No. 12, p. 242.

No. 25, *page* 71.

" Ce rachat [of liberty to industry] est le plus important
de tous les pas que l'industrie ait faits et de tous ceux
qu'elle fera par la suite.   C'était le point le plus capital
pour elle ; c'est le commencement de son existence politique que nous allons voir se développer.   Ce pas important
est désigné ordinairement sous le nom d'affranchissement
des communes."—*De l'Industrie*, 1818 ; *Hubbard*, p. 192.

Compare Comte :—" Or l'affranchissement des communes
a posé la base de ce nouvel état de choses ; il en a préparé
la possibilité, et même la nécessité."—*Op. cit.* 1820, p. 6.

No. 26, *page* 71.

" La transition qui s'opère actuellement se compose,
comme la précédente, de deux autres—l'une philosophique,
l'autre politique.   La première consiste dans le passage du
système théologique au système terrestre et positif ; la
seconde, dans le passage du régime arbitraire au régime

libéral et industriel. La révolution philosophique a déjà commencé depuis bien longtemps ; car on doit en rapporter l'origine à la culture des sciences positives, introduite en Europe par les Arabes, il y a plus de dix siècles."—*Œuvres*, 1817, vol. xix. p. 25.

"Il nous faut donc un régime transitoire, et ce régime, c'est la monarchie représentative ; celui-là seul est susceptible de nous amener paisiblement au nouvel ordre social."—*Ib.* p. 27.

". . . D'où je conclus que la classe industrielle doit continuer à gagner et envahir enfin la société tout entière."—*Ib.* 1817, vol. xviii. p. 167.

No. 27, *page* 71.

" D'ailleurs, il ne suffit pas de détruire le mensonge ; il faut à la pensée de l'homme un point d'appui, . . . depuis longtemps le vice des anciennes idées générales se faisait sentir. . . . Les esprits n'ayant plus rien de convenu entre eux, se séparèrent et devinrent ennemis ; ce fut la lutte de tous les caprices et le combat de toutes les imaginations. Au défaut d'idées communes, on se rallia à des sentiments généraux. Les passions nationales se créèrent, l'égalité et la gloire militaire enivrèrent tour à tour les esprits, et le despotisme trouva bientôt sa place. . . . Que les abstractions cèdent enfin le pas aux idées positives. . . . C'est le défaut d'idées générales qui nous a perdus, nous ne renaîtrons véritablement que par des idées générales ; les anciennes sont tombées de vétusté et ne peuvent se rajeunir, il nous en faut de nouvelles."—*Œuvres*, 1817, vol. xviii. pp. 206, 213.

No. 28, *page* 72.

Speaking of the advance made between the ninth and fifteenth centuries, he says, "La division en pouvoir spirituel et en pouvoirs temporels est la première qui se présente à l'esprit. Cette division est bonne au point qu'elle n'est susceptible d'aucune amélioration."—*Œuvres Choisies*, 1813, vol. ii. p. 197.

Cf. Comte, *op. cit.* 1820, p. 7:—"Cette division est le perfectionnement le plus capital dans l'organisation sociale qui ait été fait par les modernes."

And again:—"On a perdu de vue la grande division en pouvoir spirituel et pouvoir temporel, le principal perfectionnement que l'ancien système ait introduit dans la politique générale."—*Ib.* 1822, p. 64.

No. 29, *page* 72.

"Mais remarquez que les propriétaires, quoique inférieurs en nombre, possèdent plus de lumières que vous ; et que, pour le bien général, la domination doit être répartie dans la proportion des lumières. Regardez ce qui est arrivé en France pendant le temps que vos camarades y ont dominé, ils y ont fait naître la famine."

"Les deux grands moyens de dominer—la considération et l'argent."—*Lettres de Genève*, 1803 ; *Hubbard*, p. 135.

No. 30, *page* 72.

"La crise dans laquelle toute la population européenne se trouve engagée n'a d'autre cause que l'incohérence des idées générales. Aussitôt qu'il y aura une théorie proportionnée à l'état des lumières, tout rentrera dans l'ordre."—*Œuvres Choisies*, 1813, vol. ii. p. 241.

No. 31, *page* 72.

"La guerre actuelle est évidemment causée par l'anéantissement du clergé. Ce corps, ayant négligé l'étude des sciences physiques, a abandonné aux savants laïques le sceptre de la science ; il a perdu sa considération, et une fois avili, il a été dépouillé. La guerre durera nécessairement jusqu'à l'époque où le clergé sera réorganisé."—*Œuvres Choisies*, 1813, vol. ii. p. 27.

" . . . Le passage de l'idée de plusieurs dieux à celle d'un seul. C'est ce changement dans l'idée générale qui a été la grande cause du désordre épouvantable dans lequel le vaste Empire des Romains s'est trouvé pendant plusieurs siècles. . . . Je vais parler maintenant de l'état de crise dans lequel nous nous trouvons, et je dis que cette crise (qui est extrêmement violente, puisque toute l'Europe est en guerre . . .) est nécessairement déterminée par la plus grande cause. Or la cause qui peut agir le plus fortement sur la société est un changement, un perfectionnement dans l'idée, dans la croyance générale."—*Ib.* p. 123.

No. 82, *page* 72.

" . . . D'où il résulte que les industriels sont les chefs directs et naturels de la nation travaillante, qui est la seule à laquelle la morale, la justice et le bon sens permettent d'accorder des droits politiques. . . . Je crois que les pouvoirs politiques doivent être partagés en deux classes—les uns ayant pour objet d'administrer les intérêts moraux, et les autres de régir les intérêts physiques de la société. Les savants dans les sciences physiques et mathématiques, réunis aux artistes, doivent être chargés de l'instruction publique, ainsi que tous les travaux qui ont pour objet le perfectionnement de l'intelligence collective et individuelle des membres de la société. . . . Les cultivateurs, les fabricants et les négociants doivent être principalement chargés de diriger l'administration des intérêts physiques de la société."—*Réorganisation de la Société*, 1814 ; *Hubbard*, p. 154.

No. 83, *page* 73.

"Aujourd'hui le seul objet que puisse se proposer un penseur est de travailler à la réorganisation du système de morale, du système religieux, du système politique, en un mot, du système des idées sous quelque face qu'on les envisage."—*Œuvres Choisies*, 1813, vol. ii. p. 10.

"Messieurs, je n'ai qu'une passion, celle de pacifier l'Europe; qu'une idée, celle de réorganiser la société européenne."—*Ib.* vol. ii. p. 166.

No. 84, *page* 73.

"L'Europe a formé autrefois une société confédérative unie par des institutions communes, soumise à un gouvernement général, qui était aux peuples ce que les gouvernements nationaux sont aux individus : un pareil état de choses est le seul qui puisse tout réparer."—*Ib.* vol. ii. p. 262.

"Nous affectons un mépris superbe pour les siècles qu'on appelle du moyen âge, . . . et nous ne faisons pas attention que c'est le seul temps où le système politique de l'Europe ait été fondé sur sa véritable base, sur une organisation générale."—*Ib.* vol. ii. p. 269.

"Certes ce n'est point une vision que l'idée de lier tous les peuples européens par une institution politique, puisque pendant six siècles un pareil ordre de choses a existé, et que pendant six siècles les guerres furent plus rares et moins terribles."—*Ib.* p. 270.

No. 35, *page* 73.

" Je [Dieu] leur [prêtres] retirerais le pouvoir de parler en mon nom quand ils cesseraient d'être plus savants que le troupeau qu'ils conduiraient et qu'ils se laisseraient dominer par le pouvoir temporel."—1803 ; see *Hubbard*, p. 140.

" Pour que le clergé soit utile, il faut qu'il soit considéré. Pour qu'il soit considéré, il faut qu'il soit savant ; il faut qu'il soit le corps le plus savant."—*Œuvres Choisies*, 1808, vol. i. p. 225.

" Je vois bien clairement que le pouvoir des théologiens passera dans les mains des physiciens, et qu'il se revivifiera à cette époque."—1808 ; *ib.* vol. i. p. 226.

" Toute personne qui se présentera à l'ordination ne sera faite prêtre qu'après avoir subi un examen qui constatera qu'elle est au courant des connaissances acquises sur la physique des corps bruts et sur celle des corps organisés." —1808 ; *ib.* vol. ii. p. 28.

" L'institution commune des peuples européens se rétablira d'elle-même, et un clergé d'une instruction proportionnée aux connaissances acquises, rétablira promptement le calme en Europe en mettant un frein à l'ambition des peuples et des rois."—*Ib.* vol. ii. p. 241 ; compare p. 248.

No. 36, *page* 73.

" La conséquence de ces travaux sera la réorganisation de la société européenne, au moyen d'une institution générale commune à tous les peuples qui la composent, institution qui, suivant le degré de lumières de chacun, lui paraîtra scientifique ou religieuse, mais qui, dans tous les cas exercera une action politique positive, celle de mettre un frein à l'ambition des peuples et des rois."—*Ib.* vol. ii. p. 246.

No. 37, *page* 73.

"Le pouvoir spirituel . . . passera dans les mains d'un pape et d'un clergé physicistes."—*Ib.* vol. i. p. 244.

No. 38, *page* 73.

"Dans les environs du temple, il sera bâti des laboratoires, des ateliers et un collége."—1808; see *Hubbard*, p. 142.

No. 39, *page* 73.

"Le seul Catéchisme qui puisse être admis aujourd'hui par les peuples éclairés, sera un extrait très-succinct de l'Encyclopédie, organisatrice du physicisme. On ne fera un bon Catéchisme qu'après avoir fait une bonne Encyclopédie."—*Œuvres*, 1808, vol. i. p. 224.

No. 40, *page* 73.

"Une religion bien supérieure par sa morale au Polythéisme s'est cependant établie peu de temps après les assurances données par Cicéron. On peut avec confiance dire de même aujourd'hui qu'un système de ce genre, dont la morale sera très-supérieure à celle du Christianisme, s'établira nécessairement avant peu de temps, qu'il est le seul moyen pour nous de sortir du bourbier et d'aller en avant.   Tout pas rétrograde ne peut que nous être inutile : heureusement il nous est impossible."—*Œuvres Choisies*, 1813, vol. ii. p. 129.

"Il faut passer de la morale céleste à la morale terrestre. . . . Voilà le grand pas que va faire la civilisation : il consistera dans l'établissement de la morale terrestre et positive."—*Œuvres*, 1817, vol. xix. pp. 37, 38.

No. 41, *page* 47.

" Les qualités auxquelles ils reconnaîtront ceux que Dieu a appelés à les représenter ne seront plus d'insignifiantes vertus, telles que la chastité et la continence ; ce seront des talents, ce sera le plus haut degré de talents."—1803 ; see *Hubbard*, p. 144.

No. 42, *page* 74.

" L'obligation est imposée à chacun de donner constamment à ses forces personnelles une direction utile à l'humanité. Les bras du pauvre continueront à nourrir le riche ; mais le riche reçoit le commandement de faire travailler sa cervelle, et si sa cervelle n'est pas propre au travail, il sera bien obligé de faire travailler ses bras."—*Œuvres Choisies*, 1803, vol. i. p. 40.

No. 43, *page* 74.

" Tous les hommes travailleront ; ils se regarderont tous comme des ouvriers attachés à un atelier dont les travaux ont pour but de rapprocher l'intelligence humaine de ma divine prévoyance."—*Ib.* 1803, p. 38.

" Le moraliste doit pousser l'opinion publique à punir le propriétaire oisif en le privant de toute considération."—*Ib.* 1808, p. 221.

" Dans l'état actuel de la société, tout individu est attaché à une profession intellectuelle ou manuelle, excepté les mauvais sujets et les rentiers, classe encore plus sotte et plus méprisable, qui cherche dans la vie des jouissances obtenues sans travail."—*Ib.* 1813, vol. ii. p. 46.

No. 44, *page* 75.

We find the germ of these ideas in May, 1817, when

M. Thierry writes in the 'Industrie:'—"L'objet des associations humaines a été longtemps quelque chose d'idéal, de
vague, de métaphysique. On le voit insensiblement s'ap-
procher de sa véritable nature, qui est le bien de chacun."—
Œuvres, vol. xviii. p. 24.

No. 45, *page* 76.

"Il a existé une époque à laquelle les militaires ont dû
dominer la société; et ils ont, en effet, exercé sur elle un
grand empire. Cette époque a été celle de l'ignorance.

"Les métaphysiciens et les légistes ont dû jouer ensuite
le premier rôle; car ce sont eux qui ont mis en évidence les
vices de la féodalité, et ils ont, en effet, fixé la principale
attention de la société sur leurs discours et sur leurs écrits.
Cette époque a été celle de la demi-science."—*Ib.* vol. xxi
p. 62.

No. 46, *page* 76.

Il s'ensuit que l'expression *souveraineté par la volonté
du peuple* ne signifie rien que par opposition à *souveraineté
par la grâce de Dieu.* . . . Ces deux dogmes antagonistes
n'ont donc qu'une existence réciproque. Ils sont les restes
de la longue guerre métaphysique qui a eu lieu dans toute
l'Europe occidentale, depuis la réforme, contre les principes
politiques du régime féodal."—Between June, 1820, and
January, 1821; *Œuvres*, vol. xxi. p. 210.

"L'idée vague et métaphysique de liberté."—*Ib.* p. 16,
note.

Compare M. Comte:—"Le dogme de la souveraineté du
peuple . . . a été créé pour combattre le principe du droit
divin, base politique générale de l'ancien système."—*Op. cit.*
1822, p. 53.

No. 47, *page* 76.

"Il serait absolument imphilosophique de ne pas reconnaître l'utile et remarquable influence exercée par les légistes et les métaphysiciens, pour modifier le système féodal et théologique, et pour empêcher qu'il n'étouffât le système industriel et scientifique, dès ses premiers développements. L'abolition des justices féodales, l'établissement d'une jurisprudence moins oppressive et plus régulière, sont dus aux légistes. . . . Quant aux métaphysiciens, c'est à eux qu'on doit la réforme du XVIᵉ siècle, et l'établissement du principe de la liberté de conscience, qui a sapé dans sa base le pouvoir théologique. . . . Pour moi, je déclare que je ne conçois point du tout comment l'ancien système aurait pu se modifier, et le nouveau se développer sans l'intervention des légistes et des métaphysiciens."—*Œuvres*, vol. xxi. p. 9.

Compare Comte:—"Ce ne sont pas les légistes qui ont combiné les principes de la doctrine critique, ce sont les métaphysiciens, qui du reste forment, sous le rapport spirituel, la classe correspondante à celle des légistes sous le rapport temporel."—*Comte, op. cit.* 1822, p. 70.

No. 48, *page* 76.

"C'est évidemment par eux [les métaphysiciens] que la transition s'est opérée, au spirituel, en Angleterre et en Allemagne. En France, ce sont surtout les gens de lettres qui ont joué ce rôle. Mais, comme tous leurs principes ont été essentiellement métaphysiques, j'ai cru devoir adopter la dénomination de *métaphysiciens* de préférence à celle des *littérateurs*, comme étant à la fois plus générale et plus caractéristique."—*Œuvres*, 1820, vol. xxi. *note*, p. 81.

s

"Luther, en ébranlant dans les esprits ce vieux respect qui faisait la force du clergé, désorganisa l'Europe. La moitié des Européens s'affranchit des chaînes du papisme, c'est-à-dire, brisa le seul lien politique qui l'attachât à la grande société."—*Organisateur*, 1814; *Œuvres Choisies*, vol. ii. p. 260.

Compare Comte :—"L'attaque de Luther et de ses coréformateurs contre l'autorité pontificale, a renversé de fait le pouvoir spirituel, comme pouvoir européen, ce qui était son véritable caractère politique."—*Op. cit.* 1820, p. 10.

No. 49, *page 76.*

"Il est dans la nature de l'homme de ne pouvoir passer sans intermédiaire d'une doctrine quelconque à une autre. Cette loi s'applique bien plus impérieusement encore aux différents systèmes politiques par lesquels la marche naturelle de la civilisation oblige l'espèce humaine à passer. Ainsi, la même nécessité, qui a créé dans l'industrie l'élément d'un nouveau pouvoir temporel destiné à remplacer le pouvoir militaire, et, dans les sciences positives, l'élément d'un nouveau pouvoir spirituel appelé à succéder au pouvoir théologique, a dû développer et de mettre en activité (avant que ce changement dans l'état de la société eût commencé à devenir très-sensible) un pouvoir temporel et un pouvoir spirituel d'une nature intermédiaire, bâtarde et transitoire, dont l'unique rôle était d'opérer la transition d'un système social à l'autre.

"Pour passer du principe militaire au principe industriel, il a dû se former un principe intermédiaire, qui, en reconnaissant la suprématie du premier, assujettit cependant l'action de la force à des limitations et à des règles puisées dans l'intérêt des industriels.

"De même, pour passer du pouvoir théologique fondé sur la révélation au pouvoir scientifique fondé par la démonstration, il a dû s'établir un pouvoir moyen, qui, en admettant la supériorité de certaines croyances religieuses fondamentales, fît accorder le droit d'examen sur tous les articles secondaires.

"L'histoire nous montre que ces deux classes intermédiaires ont été, pour le temporel, celle des légistes, et, pour le spirituel, celle des métaphysiciens.

"Les légistes, qui n'étaient à l'origine que des agents des militaires, ont bientôt formé une classe distincte, qui a modifié l'action féodale par l'établissement de la jurisprudence, laquelle n'a été qu'un système organisé de barrières opposées à l'exercice de la force.

"Pareillement, les métaphysiciens, sortis d'abord du sein de la théologie, sans cesser jamais de fonder leurs raisonnements sur une base religieuse, ont modifié l'influence théologique par l'établissement du droit d'examen en matière de dogme et de morale.

"Leur action, qui a commencé principalement à la réforme du XVIᵉ siècle, s'est terminée, dans le siècle dernier, par la proclamation du principe de la liberté illimitée de conscience."—June, 1820, to January, 1821; *Œuvres*, vol. xxi. pp. 80–81.

Compare Comte:—". . . Le dogme de la liberté illimitée de conscience . . . n'est autre chose que la traduction d'un grand fait général, la décadence des croyances théologiques. Résultat de cette décadence, il a, par une réaction nécessaire, puissamment contribué à l'accélérer et à la propager. . . . il perd toute sa valeur aussitôt qu'on veut y voir une des bases de la grande réorganisation sociale."—*Op. cit.* 1822, p. 53.

No. 50, *page* 76.

"Cet intermédiaire était tellement commandé par la nature même des choses, qu'on le retrouve jusque dans la manière de traiter les questions purement scientifiques. Quel est l'astronome, le physicien, le chimiste et le physiologiste qui ne sait qu'avant de passer, dans chaque branche, des idées purement théologiques aux idées positives, l'esprit humain s'est servi pendant longtemps de la métaphysique? Chacun de ceux qui ont réfléchi sur la marche des sciences, n'est-il pas convaincu que cet état intermédiaire a été utile, et même absolument indispensable pour opérer la transition?"—*Œuvres*, vol. xxi. p. 9.

No. 51, *page* 76.

For his opinion in 1817, see above, p. 249, No. 27.

"Croyez-vous que la critique des idées théologiques et féodales faite, ou du moins terminée par les philosophes du xviiie siècle, puisse tenir lieu d'une doctrine? La société ne vit point d'idées négatives mais d'idées positives."—*Ib.* vol. xxii. p. 51. (December, 1820; see vol. xxi. p. xii.)

"Laisser périr l'ancien système sans lui en substituer un nouveau, est une idée absolument fausse. . . . Une doctrine générale doit maintenir l'ordre entre les différentes nations assez avancées pour pouvoir l'adopter, aussi bien qu'entre les divers individus d'une nation unique."—*Ib.* p. 53.

"Sous ce rapport la formation de la doctrine qui doit servir de base au système industriel, comme l'ancienne a servi de base au système féodal, est d'une nécessité tout-à-fait urgente."—*Ib.* p. 54.

No. 52, *page* 78.

We may even observe an occasional verbal similarity; for instance, Saint-Simon writes, in 1819, "Il n'y a d'hommes utiles que les *savants*, les *artistes* et les *artisans*, et de travaux utiles que les leurs" (*Œuvres Choisies*, vol. ii. p. 369); and Comte, in 1820, "Je laisse à juger si l'organisation du nouveau système est une chose urgente, et si les *artistes*, les *savants* et les *artisans* ne commettent pas la plus grande faute en s'endormant à cet égard." (*Op. cit.* p. 19.)

The use of the word "spirituel" to signify speculative is also borrowed from Saint-Simon. M. Littré found it necessary to explain its peculiar meaning to his readers. ('Auguste Comte,' p. 153.)

No. 53, *page* 79.

In the Preface to the 'Science de l'Homme,' 1813, he wrote, "Je déclare en y entrant que je suis prêt à quitter la direction de l'entreprise, que mon plus grand désir est de voir une personne plus capable que moi s'en charger, et que je deviendrai dès ce moment pour elle un collaborateur qu'elle emploiera comme elle le jugera à propos. En attendant l'heureux jour où je me trouverai débarrassé de cette tâche (infiniment au-dessus de mes forces), voici la marche que je suivrai pour la remplir le moins mal qu'il me sera possible."—*Œuvres Choisies*, vol. ii. p. 11.

In the 'Système Industriel' he continued, "Aucun philosophe ne se présentant pour obéir à cette grande mission, que l'état de la civilisation met réellement à l'ordre du jour, j'ai osé m'en charger. Je serai heureux si mon travail peut déterminer à s'en occuper un philosophe positif plus habile, ou si, bientôt, je puis avoir assez avancé l'entreprise pour pouvoir la remettre entre les mains des savants, ce qui est l'objet de tous mes vœux."—*Œuvres*, vol. xxii. p. 59.

END OF THE APPENDICES.

PRINTED BY TAYLOR AND CO.,
LITTLE QUEEN STREET, LINCOLN'S INN FIELDS.